KV-060-895

CITIZENS BY RIGHT

Citizenship education in primary schools

Reva Klein

Trentham Books and Save the Children

Stoke on Trent, UK and Sterling, USA

Trentham Books Limited

Westview House   22883 Quicksilver Drive
734 London Road   Sterling
Oakhill   VA 20166-2012
Stoke on Trent   USA
Staffordshire
England ST4 5NP

© 2001 Save the Children

All rights reserved. No part of this publication may be reproduced or transmitted in any form or by any means, electronic or mechanical including photocopying, recording or any information storage or retrieval system, without prior permission in writing from the publishers.

First published 2001

British Library Cataloguing-in-Publication Data
A catalogue record for this book is available from the British Library ·

ISBN 1 85856 220 1

Designed and typeset by Trentham Print Design Ltd., Chester and printed in Great Britain by Bemrose Shafron (Printers) Ltd., Chester.

Acknowledgement
I would like to thank the following people for their cooperation, support and guidance:

Nicky Road, Assistant Programme Director, Save the Children Lina Fajerman, Tina Hyder, Sue Emerson and Bharti Mepani of Save the Children's Younger Children's Team.

The participating teachers and pupils at Torriano, Argyle, Beckford and Gospel Oak Primary Schools.

Gillian Klein, my editor, for her encouragement and good humour.

I especially wish to thank Ali Browlie for her invaluable contributions to the text and for undertaking the extensive background research for this publication. My thanks also to Don Harrison for contributing the text for chapter 6 on global citizenship.

6000486966

WITHDRAWN

 University of
Hertfordshire

College Lane, Hatfield, Herts. AL10 9AB

Learning and Information Services
de Havilland Campus Learning Resources Centre, Hatfield

For renewal of Standard and One Week Loans,
please visit the web site **http://www.voyager.herts.ac.uk**

This item must be returned or the loan renewed by the due date.
The University reserves the right to recall items from loan at any time.
A fine will be charged for the late return of items.

CITIZENS BY RIGHT

Citizenship education in primary schools

Contents

FOREWORD

Save the Children is the UK's leading international children's charity, working to create a better future for children. We are committed to working towards enabling all children to have a happy, healthy and secure childhood. In a world where children are denied basic human rights, we are exploring with them ways of realising children's rights in all contexts.

When we developed the idea of exploring children's rights through the introduction of citizenship into the national curriculum, we were genuinely seeking answers to such questions as: Can children's rights be introduced to young children so that the concept conveys real meaning to them? Do children in the UK see the relevance of this knowledge? And how will it inform their actions? The result was the Camden Project, an experiment which brought together two subjects many teachers may never have embraced singly, let alone together: children's rights and citizenship. This book documents the project as it evolved in four primary schools and offers guidance to primary teachers who wish to follow what proved to be a highly successful approach.

We were also interested in exploring what our approach meant for the adults working with children – particularly teachers who are required to plan lessons carefully and to be clear about what the learning outcomes will be. We asked teachers to work with us on a process of involving children in the planning. We asked them to base the programme of work on things that had particular relevance to the group of children in their class. We were asking them to work differently. We saw the introduction of citizenship into the curriculum as an important and ideal opportunity to work with the children on issues of real concern to them, based on a concept of rights.

We made it clear that Save the Children would give support, information and guidance, the members of its Younger Children's team providing training and working alongside the teachers. But it would be up to each teacher to shape the work in their class according to their own interests, inclinations and intuition.

The teachers drew on their considerable creative thinking to find approaches to teaching children about their rights that were appropriate to their classes and were in keeping with their own education philosophy and with the ethos of the school. Each independently came to the conclusion, which we share, that rights had to be *experienced* as well as *learned* formally and cognitively. The content and spirit of the subject demands it. It is, as Reva Klein says, 'the nature of the beast'.

And beastly that process could seem at first. How do you, as a teacher, loosen the tight reins that are part and parcel of ensuring structured lessons that address attainment targets and mapped out schemes of work, never mind manageable behaviour? How do you allow children to share the responsibility of holding those reins by giving them the right to say what they want to learn and how they want to learn it?

But giving children the opportunity to discover and exercise their rights proved to be as exhilarating and productive a process for the teachers as for the pupils. It enabled both to experience the excitement of spontaneous teaching and learning. Teachers saw that the project produced unexpected fringe benefits: the children showed more respect towards each other and an increased interest in human rights generally. And it gave teachers the scope to reassess their own practice, their expectations of their pupils and their ideas about classroom management and control.

Within the story of the Camden Project, the book interweaves factual information on relevant human rights legislation and strategies for use in the classroom. It suggests, too, how a rights approach to citizenship can and should be expanded to encompass a global perspective. We hope that these theoretical and practical ideas will stimulate teachers to look at and experience with their pupils the complex but compelling theme of children's rights.

At an INSET to disseminate the learning to other teachers and schools in the education authority, the Camden PSHE adviser told one of the teachers that what she had described sounded like an example of an excellent PSHE activity. The teacher replied that the difference was that she was doing it from a children's right perspective and that this perspective had changed how she viewed the capabilities of the children in her class and also her own starting point. Involving children in the development process had paid off. We hope this difference will be apparent to you when you read this account and that it will give you the confidence and enthusiasm to try it for yourselves.

Nicky Road
Younger Children's Team
Save the Children
August 2001

Chapter One

CHILDREN'S RIGHTS AS A KEY TO CITIZENSHIP

HOW DO THEY FIT TOGETHER?

Citizenship helps students understand what it means to belong to communities, to understand the language of morality, of rights and responsibilities towards others... Citizenship engages students because it encourages them to reflect on and understand their own experiences... In particular, it is one curriculum area in which the mutual exploration of problems is rather more important than learning a set of right answers. Don Rowe, Citizenship Foundation, from an article in the *Times Educational Supplement*, July 1997

In western classical civilisation, the notion of citizenship was connected to belonging to a defined community, usually a city state. The concept broadened to encompass citizens belonging to entities beyond national boundaries through the writings of philosophers, including Aristotle, and by the multi-ethnicity of the Roman Empire.

In the English language and in the United Kingdom and throughout its former empire, citizenship meant an exclusive affiliation with Britain and its culture. Citizenship was defined by nationality and brought with it notions of national unity and pride. A century ago, British textbooks with names like *True Patriotism*, *Brave Citizens* and *Good Citizenship* were used in schools. The latter included a lesson in which children were asked how many of them could recite the first verse of God Save the Queen. The aim of the lesson was 'to inculcate loyalty to the Monarch and to Christ.'

A teachers' manual published in the 1920s advised teachers not to 'say too much about slavery; pass lightly over the right to revolution.' During those politically and economically unstable interwar years, the government was intent on creating obedient subjects for the future, rather than citizens in their own right with their own rights.

By the 1960s and 1970s, civics lessons in secondary schools were little more than a user's guide to the workings of democracy, Parliament and the legal system. It was characterised by an unquestioning acceptance of the delivery of the constitution, police and the judiciary. Unsurprisingly, it was a tedious subject for children and teachers alike.

There was little apparent activity that could be identified as citizenship education in primary schools at that time, although changes in teaching practices brought about by the Plowden Report introduced more interactive methods and class participation.

Towards the end of the last century, influential educationalists and others in public service in the UK began to talk about citizenship education again, largely in response to declining interest in the processes of democracy. The parliamentary Speaker's Commission on Citizenship sparked a debate and civic action towards greater public understanding of and interest in citizenship on local, national and (to a limited extent) international levels.

Any debate about the nature of citizenship necessarily involves discussion about how people, particularly children in schools, learn to be citizens. So the past few years have seen increased professional debate about what education for citizenship means and involves within the context of the national curriculum and classroom application.

Citizenship appeared as a non-statutory cross-curricular theme in the watershed national curriculum introduced in the 1988 Education Reform Act. Defining the need for some kind of sociopolitical dimension to young people's learning in state schools led to a government body being set up to review possibilities for introducing a more coherent citizenship syllabus in schools. Led by Professor Bernard Crick, the working party produced a report in 1998 entitled *Education for citizenship and the teaching of democracy in schools*.

The end result of the report is the compulsory introduction of education for citizenship in secondary schools in England from 2002. Although primary children do not have to study citizenship as a discrete subject, it must appear as a recognisable strand within personal, social and health education. The framework encourages young children to question the workings of the society that they are members of and to express their opinions with confidence. Curriculum 2000 states that pupils should be taught:

- to talk and write about their opinions and explain their views on issues that affect themselves and society and

- why and how rules and laws are made and enforced, why different rules are needed in different situations and how to take part in making and changing rules.

A far cry indeed from the passive, jingoistic notion of citizenship with which our grandparents grew up.

The Camden Project

In this account of the project, *Citizens by Right* brings together two recent educational trends that have until recently been considered peripheral to the curriculum: citizenship education and human rights education.

Save the Children UK supported the initiative and is a partner in the publication of this book. As a leading children's rights organisation in the UK with a practice base in over 60 of the world's poorest countries, Save the Children has a wealth of experience in working with schools. For the Camden Project, it gave support to the teachers by way of resources, training and guidance from four members of its younger children's team.

The four schools in the project applied to take part and were selected by Nicky Road, SC's Assistant Programme Director, working alongside Gill Morris, Camden's PHSE and Citizenship Adviser. Among the criteria for selection was that the schools had a school council, a PTA and a willingness to allow the project to choose an age group that ensured that there was a spread across the schools, for the purpose of testing how the brief worked with different ages. Each school was asked to put together developmentally appropriate programmes of work for rights-based citizenship education during 1998-1999.

At Gospel Oak, the reception class was involved. They explored feelings, conflicts and friendships through story, puppets and photography.

Beckford School's Year One class also used feelings and story as a way to approach rights issues.

Year Three children at Torriano Juniors looked at the UN Convention and devised role-plays to illustrate their rights.

Argyle School's Year Fives looked at the philosophical aspect of rights and brought their own experiences from countries around the world into discussions.

The purposes of the book are to:

- share the findings and explore the issues that arose from the experience

- stimulate discussion and debate among teachers about citizenship education and teaching children's rights

- encourage teachers to consider a children's rights approach to citizenship education

The reasons SC initiated the project were:

- to develop work on and analyse the potential for children's rights education within the context of the new framework for citizenship education in England

- to work alongside and support teachers on a project that put children at the centre of their own rights

- to listen to what children themselves had to say about their rights and what participation meant for them

- to explore ways of enabling young children to develop an understanding of children's rights and citizenship

We hope that teachers reading this book will feel encouraged to use the UN Convention as a key teaching document and that they will try out the learning activities in their classrooms.

There is a clear interface between children's/human rights and citizenship education. Rights and responsibilities feature prominently in the Curriculum 2000's framework for personal, social and health and citizenship education (QCA and DfEE, 1999), alongside other elements of citizenship such as moral

Your Bill of Rights

education, social inclusion and sustainable development. By bringing rights education into citizenship in a carefully thought-out programme, teachers are:

> affirming children's rights to participation in their school and the wider community

> facilitating the development of children's self-esteem and confidence

> acknowledging the importance of the whole school environment on education for citizenship.

The programmes that the Camden teachers developed with their SC colleagues all addressed the aims of affirming children's rights to participation in school and society, developing their self-esteem and appreciating the importance of a whole school approach to rights.

A new way of looking at citizenship

Equipping children with the critical and cognitive tools to communicate their points of view and make decisions for themselves signifies a seismic philosophical shift in education in this country. Where schools have for many years avoided discussing controversial issues and children were firmly put in their place as passive recipients of knowledge, 'good education' now is being interpreted through the new national curriculum orders for citizenship education as empowering young children to not only understand the concept of rights but to learn what their rights are and what their role is in ensuring those rights are met in order to fulfil their own educational potential. The message inherent in the curriculum framework is that citizenship is not just about preparing children to become active citizens when they are older; it's about acknowledging that they are part of society today, that they are aware of the world in which they live and that they are eager to take their place in it.

As the Qualifications and Curriculum Authority advisory group on citizenship education put it in 1998:

> *Some might regard the whole of primary school education as pre-citizenship, certainly pre-political; but this is mistaken. Children are already forming, through learning and discussion, concepts of fairness and attitudes to the law, to rules, to decision-making, to authority, to their local environment and social responsibility etc... All this can be encouraged, guided and built upon.*

But the framework also emphasises the importance of preparing children to 'become informed, active, responsible citizens.' The stress is on respect for the law, responsibility and making a contribution to community life. Andrew West of SC argues that we must move on from seeing citizenship as linked to nationality and voting – and thus having an age threshold – to what should be lifelong citizenship. Citizenship education can only make sense, he suggests, if children's citizenship and rights are acknowledged and given an equal, albeit differentiated weighting from adults.

What does the citizenship curriculum have to do with rights?

The framework for citizenship education and PSHE at Key Stages 1 and 2 sets out clear guidelines for promoting the development of children's confidence and responsibility, making the most of their abilities and preparing them to play an active role as citizens.

The groundwork for understanding the concept of rights and responsibilities and preparation for playing an active role as citizens is laid down at Key Stage 1, where pupils should be taught to:

- recognise what they like and dislike, what is fair and unfair and what is right and wrong

- share their opinions on things that matter to them and explain their views

- recognise, name and deal with their feelings in a positive way

- think about themselves, learn from their experiences and recognise what they are good at.

The focus on the self is taken further at Key Stage 2, when they should be taught to:

- talk and write about their opinions and explain their views on issues that effect themselves and society

- recognise their worth as individuals by identifying positive things about themselves and their achievements, seeing their mistakes, making amends and setting personal goals

- face new challenges positively by collecting information, looking for help, making responsible choices and taking action.

At this stage, there should also be preparation for active citizenship as children are being taught:

- to research, discuss and debate topical issues, problems and events

- why and how rules and laws are made and enforced, why different rules are needed in different situations and how to take part in making and changing rules

- to realise the consequences of anti-social and aggressive behaviours, such as bullying and racism, on individuals and communities

- that there are different kinds of responsibilities, rights and duties at home, at school and in the community, and that these can sometimes conflict with each other

- to reflect on spiritual, moral, social and cultural issues, using imagination to understand other people's experiences

- to resolve differences by looking at alternatives, making decisions and explaining choices.

Think global

A shortcoming in the official government perception of citizenship education in England is the weak intercultural and international focus, contrary to the 1985 Council of Europe recommendations (see below). Children perceive themselves as global citizens. Think of James Joyce's Stephen Daedalus, the young protagonist in *A Portrait of the Artist as a Young Man* or Sue Townsend's eponymous Adrian Mole who, while they don't have an awful lot in common, both place themselves squarely in the universe, after listing the name of their street, their town, their country, continent etc – in a way that young adolescents do, everywhere. While children are very much of their own neighbourhoods, cultures and friendship groups, they are also hungry for information about and connections with places, people and ideas outside their worlds. The advent of information technology has made this hunger easier to satiate in some ways and, in other ways, has fuelled it even more.

Despite children's wider awareness of the world, the Framework for Education for Citizenship has little to offer teachers and their pupils for building up an internationalist approach to citizenship education. For example, the provision at Key Stage Two for 'using imagination to understand other people's experiences' misses the opportunity to point teachers in multicultural and

from *Partners in Rights*. SC, 2000

international directions. In schools where the pupil population speaks 20 or more different languages, who are 'other people?' And who are they in schools at the other end of the spectrum, where there is no cultural diversity? We will look later at how to engender a global perspective on citizenship.

What does the UN Convention on the Rights of the Child have to do with citizenship?

The United Nations adopted the Convention on the Rights of the Child in 1989 and since then all but two of the 193 member states (the United States and Somalia) have ratified it. Following Britain's signing of the Convention in 1991, there has been growing recognition of the need to ensure that its articles are enacted within the education system. The principles embodied in the Convention lend themselves to the development of:

codes of behaviour in schools

the organisation and management of schools

a planning framework for the curriculum

Here's what the Convention says about education for citizenship. Article 29 states:

....the education of the child shall be directed to...the preparation of the child for responsible life in a free society, in the spirit of understanding, peace, tolerance, equality of sexes and friendship among all peoples, ethnic, national and religious groups and persons of indigenous origin.

The Convention has been adopted by Save the Children and UNICEF as their manifesto for educational action. Its philosophy as an internationally agreed document of rights for all children (with provisos on certain sections by individual states, including the UK) sets a challenge for educational structures which are discriminatory or non-inclusive. Here are some key points from the Convention that informed the way teachers and SC team leaders approached the Camden Project.

Article 2 emphasises that all rights apply to all children and that it is the State's obligation to protect children from any form of discrimination.

Article 12 provides for a child's participation in decisions affecting him or her (assuming they are capable of forming their own views) and the right to express their views freely in all matters affecting them, including the right to be heard in any judicial or administrative proceedings affecting them.

Article 13 refers to a child's right to obtain and make known information and to express their views, unless this violates the rights of others.

Article 14 calls for freedom of thought, conscience and religion. Children should be considered people in their own right.

Article 28 upholds the child's right to education and the state's duty to ensure that, at the very minimum, primary education is compulsory and free of charge. Children's dignity must be respected in the enforcement of school discipline.

Article 29 states that the education of the child should be directed to the development of their personality, talents and mental and physical abilities and to the preparation of the child for responsible life in a free society. Education should strive to foster children's respect for basic human rights and to develop respect for the child's own cultural and national values and those of others.

Article 42 gives a clear mandate to educators to develop methods which help children learn about their rights by appropriate and active means.

What other legislative frameworks support the rights of children and their knowledge of them?

The Human Rights Act 1998, which came into force in October 2000, has a number of relevant articles within it, among them:

Article 2: The right to life. A legal opinion obtained a few years ago suggests that the right of parents to withdraw children from aspects of sex education could potentially breach the child's right to life by preventing the child from receiving life-saving information on HIV/Aids.

Article 5: The right to liberty and security. This could be interpreted as the duty of schools to ensure children's freedom from bullying and other aggressive behaviour.

Article 8: The right to respect for private and family life. This includes the right to respect for physical integrity. Could cover breaches of privacy, ie, access to school records, or breaches of confidentiality in pupils' disclosures to teachers or other staff including counsellors and education welfare officers.

Article 9: Freedom of thought, conscience and religion. Related to Article 14 of the UN Convention on the Rights of the Child. This conflicts with education legislation prohibiting children themselves to opt out of religious education and worship in schools, which only parents have the right to exercise.

Article 10: Freedom of expression. This could mean that schools that ban jewellery, certain hair styles, studs, badges, etc. (except on grounds of safety in certain circumstances) may be breaching children's rights. This Article and the preceding one would make a ban on girls wearing trousers to school in breach of the Act.

The 1985 Council of Europe Recommendations on *Teaching and Learning about Human Rights in Schools* makes useful points for teachers wishing to create a focus on rights in their classrooms. The following excerpt encapsulates its approach:

> *The study of human rights in schools should lead to an understanding of, and sympathy for, the concepts of justice, equality, freedom, peace, dignity, rights and democracy. Such understanding should be both cognitive and based on experience and feelings.*

The Council of Europe Recommendations also highlight the importance of learning and experiencing human rights as part of children's social and political education, involving 'intercultural and international understanding'.

Age is no barrier to introducing human rights, either, according to the Council of Europe:

> *Concepts associated with human rights can, and should, be acquired from an early stage. For example, the non-violent resolution of conflict and respect for other people can already be experienced within the life of a pre-school or primary class.* (Appendix suggestion 1.2 in Human rights in the school curriculum).

What we will see in the Camden Project is how teachers facilitated understanding and experiences around the themes of human rights through a variety of methods. While some were more successful than others, they all functioned as catalysts to thinking in different ways about children's interactions with their peers, with adults and with the structures and rules that circumscribe their world and beyond.

Chapter Two

TEACHING RIGHTS: CONTENT

'Everyone's got rights. Whether you're black or brown or white, you've got the right to play with anybody you want.' Five year old boy, Gospel Oak School.

Save the Children designed the project before the Crick Report on education for citizenship was published, which makes their parallels all the more interesting. Both Bernard Crick's working party and Save the Children were committed to helping build children's confidence, facilitating their understanding of the concepts of rights and responsibilities and the distinctions between them and providing them with a voice to express their views.

There are a few differences in approach, however. Save the Children's Camden Project was rooted in the belief that teachers are the best judge of how to achieve these aims. They know their pupils, they know their schools and they have vast reserves of creativity and imagination to bring to the job of communicating ideas. Following a curricular framework, therefore, isn't necessary or even desirable.

For that reason, the project was deliberately non-prescriptive in how rights education should be delivered. In addition, a priority of SC is encouraging children to develop a sense of awareness and connectedness with global issues as well as with what is going on at the community and national levels, something that is not highlighted in the framework.

Training and Planning

To help prepare teachers for the task ahead, SC held a one day training session, where all the teachers involved and SC team members came together, as well as Camden LEA's Personal, Social and Health Education advisor. A range of issues was covered. Along with being briefed on the SC approach to children's rights and citizenship, teachers were given a summary of key points of the UN Convention on the Rights of the Child and on education for citizenship. Each teacher was asked to identify the skills and attitudes towards citizenship they would like the children to acquire and the activities that might be employed to achieve them.

A further planning session was held, bringing together teacher(s) and their SC team members to map out their strategies. Throughout the project, time was given to debriefing after each session to discuss how things went and what the next step would be. For some schools, the project became an organic process that changed as the teacher and SC worker felt necessary, often led by the wishes of the children themselves.

The Camden Project was an interesting and, for some of the teachers, definitive teaching experience. Their awareness of the children's grasp of issues around fairness and rights was progressively bolstered as the project developed. They found that their pupils were keen to explore the notion of their place in society, particularly in terms of children's legal rights, initially for themselves and, as the project progressed, as it applied to others.

What transpired were different approaches to the issues adopted by each of the teachers, dictated by the age groups they were working with and by their own interpretations. Three of the schools ran the project as one session per week over the course of ten weeks; at Beckford, it was run as an intensive, three day pro-gramme. The strengths and weaknesses of their approach were identified by each of the teachers.

What follows is a description of:

how those approaches addressed key issues in the project

how they were implemented

and how the teachers and SC team perceived them.

How do you explain the concept of rights?

Teaching children the facts about rights – their own, those of others, about organisations engaged in upholding human rights and about documents and legal frameworks such as the UN Convention and the Human Rights Act – is an important function of citizenship education and one which, if done well, can have life-long effects. To learn that there are laws and conventions that define and describe the rights to which they are entitled can be an empowering experience for children.

But of course there are developmental realities that have to be taken into consideration when we talk about teaching rights and citizenship to young children. Piaget believed, for example, that before the age of seven children don't have the empathic skills that allow them to put themselves in another person's position and understand other points of view. Until that age, his theory goes, they are essentially egocentric and tend to impute egocentric motives to others, too. So when another child bumps into them in the playground they will assume that it was deliberate rather than an accident. Although more recent research, particularly by Margaret Donaldson, has debunked his theory, and work with Persona Dolls has shown that children as young as two can be deeply empathic, children need to be given tangible contexts if they are to comprehend the rights and responsibilities of the individual in relation to others.

Any attempt to deal with the concepts of society, citizenship and human rights must be framed in developmentally appropriate contexts.

Rights and issues around the democratic process are already in the ether and in the curriculum of all schools, even if they are generally implicit rather than explicit. They are what fuels school councils, they are recurring themes in circle time, they are there for the taking in the morality of stories that are read in literacy hour – whether in fantasy stories like Cinderella or in stories more rooted in reality like *Journey to Jo'burg*. And of course they are ever-present in history and geography studies.

Getting rights right

A children's or human rights approach to education is much more than teaching about rights: it is about teaching and learning *for* rights and about recognising and respecting children's rights within school. Learning for rights means working towards achieving them rather than offering the subject as an area of knowledge. It is, essentially, an approach to education, encompassing the curriculum, classroom organisation and teaching methodology as well as the school's ethos and organisation. The ethos and values explicit and implicit in the Citizenship Education Framework recognises the need to put children at the centre of their own learning and invites this holistic approach to teaching children's rights.

Teachers hold different views on how early the concept of rights can be understood by children. Even for adults, human rights are not as clear-cut as they might appear at first glance, let alone for children. It's not difficult to become confused about what the notion of rights mean in a world where freedom of the individual can impact negatively on others. In America, people have the right to own a gun but in many public places are prohibited from smoking. In this country, parents' rights to good education for their children or appropriate health care are regularly compromised because of where they live and how much they earn.

Teachers may be concerned that citizenship education and teaching about rights are areas that are too difficult or irrelevant to young children. But there are clear conceptual parallels between what happens in the wider political world and the events that children experience on a day to day basis in the classroom.

From an early age, children are putting together their world view from an assortment of sources. They need help in making sense of them as well as in rehearsing how to debate and discuss their ideas and views. Citizens aren't born. Children need to practice being citizens while being seen and treated in this way. Annabelle Dixon, former Lucy Cavendish research fellow in citizenship studies, emphasised the importance of identifying opportunities for developing citizenship education with young children when she wrote:

> Being absorbed in the immediate work situation, it is not always easy to see how the encouragement of friendly and co-operative attitudes among children as members of a group might be contributing, in its small way, to the very nature of society as we would wish it to be. The task for early years educators is to be able to recognise the issues and, when they arise in the world of the young child, to help children develop the skills that will enable them to deal with these issues.
> Annabelle Dixon, 1998

Seizing opportunities for discussion

The following are some broader human rights issues that are linked with examples of children's everyday experiences and can be used to illustrate the concepts in ways that pupils can relate to.

Prejudice
Children calling each other names based on racial or cultural differences or because they look or act differently from the 'norm.'

Discrimination
Excluding others from play or refusing to work with them.

Resource distribution
Arguing over materials, going without something. The positive flipside is sharing what is available.

Conflict
Fighting and arguments, aggressive behaviour.

Peace
Personal assertiveness, conflict resolution.

Environmental awareness
Negative example: using materials unwisely, wastefulness, dropping litter. Positive example: putting tops back on pens, involvement in poster campaigns to keep the school clean.

Interdependence
Sharing and working together with others.

Mediation
Negotiating to find a solution to a conflict.

Power
One child or group being valued more and having more control than another, or the hierarchical structure of the classroom and school.

Choice and action
Children deciding for themselves what activities to take part in or being involved in planning what they would like to do.

For the Camden teachers, discussions about the value of starting to learn from examples of specific rights or the lack of them opened the way to explore various vehicles for bringing those examples into the classroom.

Grasping notions
The teachers of the two older groups of primary children in the Camden Project felt that their pupils could grasp the notion of rights by ranking them in order of importance and classifying types of rights into groups like *participation*, *protection* and *provision*. This kind of learning activity can contribute to understanding but has its limitations, too. If children aren't clear from the outset that rights are socially determined principles – as distinct from personal desires or physical needs – they're likely to come up with the idea of rights being about things like staying up late, having a mobile phone or eating whatever they like.

Dividing rights into categories isn't necessarily easy. Specific rights can fall into any number of categories. The right to education, for instance, can be perceived as both social *provision* and children's *participation*. The challenge to teachers is to break down the adult-conceived language of United Nations instruments into child-friendly terms and visual representations.

An alternative approach to learning about rights is to explore with pupils their understanding in particular areas, moving towards a vocabulary of rights. For example, project work on homes and families can be extended to discuss who cares for children, leading to the conclusion that children should have care and family protection as a right by dint of being children. This can be taken further by asking what happens if children aren't able to claim such a right. Is it then just a matter of parents' goodwill or adherence to personal principles? With such an approach, pupils should begin to grasp the notion that a right is guaranteed by others according to an accepted standard.

The UN Convention at a glance

Whichever approach teachers choose to adopt – from the general to the particular or vice versa – they can refer back to the international agreements for guidance. They should obtain their own copies of these documents if they aren't readily available in the school. The following are two simplified versions of the UN Convention designed for use in primary schools.

Article 3: Grown ups should do their best for you.

Article 6: You have the right to life.

Article 12: Grown ups must listen to what children say.

Article 13: You can say what you think.

Article 14: You have a right to your religion.

Article 15: You can make friends with whomever you chose

Article 16: You can have your own private things (diary)

Article 17: No one must tell lies about you

Article 18: Parents must take care of their children

Article 19: Children must not be hurt

Article 20: Someone must look after children

Article 22: Refugee children must be looked after

Article 23: Disabled children need to have special care

Article 24: Children must have medicine if they are sick

No one should hurt you

Article 25 You should have food, clothes and a place to live

Article 28: All children should go to school and have an education

Article 31: Children have a right to play

Article 32: Children shouldn't have to do work that hurts them

Article 33: You should be safe from drugs

Adapted by Lina Fajerman, Save the Children Younger Children's Team

All children have rights to:

equality
survival and development
name and identity
freedom of expression
freedom of religion
freedom of association
privacy
family care and protection
health care and education
adequate standard of living
education
protection from harmful work
protection from drugs
protection from abuse and violence
justice

Some children have additional rights:

special protection for refugee children
special care and education for disabled children
special recovery for mistreated children

The first internationally agreed statement of children's rights, the 1924 League of Nations *Declaration*, was much simpler in its language and remit, particularly when calling for provision for children's basic needs. The language of the Convention is a far more sophisticated and complex document, covering as it does so many areas of rights for children.

The challenge to teachers is to communicate the provisions of the Convention 'by appropriate and active means.' The four Camden schools provide good examples of different ways of doing this, working from a foundation of looking at issues around personal identity and protection.

Every child has the right to an opinion

The United Nations Convention on the Rights of the Child

TEACHING *ABOUT* RIGHTS

Teaching children the facts about rights – their own, those of others, about organisations engaged in upholding human rights and about documents and legal frameworks such as the UN Convention and the Human Rights Act – is an important function of citizenship education and one which, if done well, can have lifelong effects. To learn that there are laws and conventions that define and describe the rights to which they are entitled can be an empowering experience for children. Children need an understanding of the rights to which everyone is entitled and they need to be able to recognise when those rights are being denied.

To many in the west, human rights issues tend to concern people 'over there': those living under brutal regimes or in conflict situations or in dire situations of mental and physical abuse. However, there is no country in the world at present where children are secure and protected in all their rights. For example, a Save the Children report on the state of children's rights in Britain, compiled as part of a report to the United Nations, found that even in this country, children's voices are being ignored. Here are two examples:

> *There's a complaints system here. You can say 'can I make a complaint?' and they say 'what is it?' and you tell them and they say 'no, it's not serious enough'.* A child in secure accommodation.
>
> *I must have been threatened about a thousand times.* School child talking about a teacher.

There are innumerable examples of children's rights being ignored in this country, in the United States and throughout the developed world. The fact that one third of all children in this country live below the poverty line underlines the scale of in-

---

OUR RIGHTS

This is a simple but useful way of initiating discussions about the rights teachers and pupils think they should have.

Working in groups of three or four, individuals should start by preparing a list of ten rights which they believe everyone in their group should have. Lists are compared and the group agrees, through consensus or voting, on ten rights for their group. Each individual can choose one point that they feel particularly strongly about and map out the implications if everyone had that right.

Discussions can focus on the reasons behind any differences in opinion and acknowledge that sometimes rights can conflict with each other: one person's right may be someone else's infringement.

---

equality, lack of choice and muted voices that millions of children and their families live with.

Rights in the curriculum

Rights issues are already present across the curriculum, but usually in an implicit rather than explicit form. Teachers usually discuss the morals and ethics represented in a story in literacy hour, for example, in much the same way as Camden project teachers at Beckford School did when looking at questions of fairness and equality in the story of Cinderella.

In history, children have the option of learning about human rights struggles around the world. As well as learning about the leaders of liberation movements such as Martin Luther King,

Mahatma Gandhi and the like, they may be taught 'history from below' to highlight the actions of groups of people often omitted from history books. The events leading up to the Universal Declaration of Human Rights and the Convention on the Rights of the Child are fertile areas for leading into or complementing work on citizenship education.

Geography offers opportunities to learn how people's rights are met in different places through, for instance, development education: the basic right to food and clean water, interdependence and sustainable development. Older children may explore the rights issues associated with tourism, refugees, land, working conditions and the environment. Where these reflect the opinions of different groups of people, decision-making exercises can be used which are in themselves activities for citizenship, offering insights into understanding differing viewpoints within a single community.

In the Camden Project, there was a predictable dichotomy in pedagogic approaches dictated by the year groups involved, based on age. The two schools that had involved older children (Torriano and Argyle) introduced the project by drawing on facts and exploring meanings. The teachers and SC workers felt that the Year 3 and Year 5 pupils were not only old enough to be able to deal with the data that was required but also that it was a good way of launching the subject before moving into more artistic and experiential learning experiences. The two schools in which a reception and Year 1 class were the participants (Beckford and Gospel Oak) opted to use a highly experiential way of dealing with the issues, with emotional literacy as the vehicle.

Starting from square one
Natasha Ewing, who taught a Year 3 class at Torriano School, led discussions with her pupils on what rights means in reality.

We talked about the fact that, yes, we have rights to say what we feel and think, but we also questioned about whether there are boundaries. For example, should you have the right to stay home from school? to speak out whenever you want? If you have the right to voice your views, how can you ensure that others do, too? We discussed the belief that there are times and places for rights to be expressed and then asked: what are they?

From there, they deconstructed the UN Convention into bite-sized bits. Lina Fajerman of SC adapted salient points of the Convention to make it understandable to seven year olds and then had them prioritise the rights according to their own frames of reference.

Because the children wanted to know more about children's rights in other countries, Natasha asked Lina to compile some statements on children's rights from around the world and pupils were then asked to categorise them in terms of what you should be protected from and what you should be allowed to do. This was followed by a discussion on why they put them into the groups they did.

The way we worked was a good example of reflective practice. Natasha and I discussed things a lot in the planning stages and also in post-mortems after every session. The reflection that the project allowed is so important and something that's become increasingly rare for classroom teachers. Lina Fajerman, SC

Another activity involved distinguishing between needs and wants. Pairs of children divided picture cards illustrating these ideas into piles. This exercise not only worked to clarify these two terms but also encouraged children to argue their position and cooperate.

I don't think I'd have thought before about teaching children's rights because I didn't know much about it before. This has made me aware that children can go through life without knowing about rights – like me before the project – or that they can know about rights and take them too literally. It's important to present the issues in an informative way that clarifies where the boundaries lie. Natasha Ewing

At Argyle School, where 91% of the children speak English as an additional language and a large proportion of them are refugees, the three teachers involved in the project and SC's Bharti Mepani looked at how children's rights could be woven into the curriculum. They decided to start with the UN Convention itself, breaking down its meaning to aid the children's understanding and looking at the distinction between rights and privileges.

In the most overtly factual exercise of the entire project, the teachers spent a session with their classes on the history of the Convention, using a timeline to put important events in its development into sequence. In another session, they carved the charter up into points and put the points onto cards. The children divided into small groups and put the cards in order of importance. When they next met, they discussed each groups' order of priority of things like the right to privacy, education, relaxation, feeling safe, expression of opinions. Overleaf is a timeline that gives teachers an overview of human rights history and that they can edit and adapt for primary use.

In these discussions, the disparities of the children's own experiences from around the world were highlighted, with the focus on how their rights were or were not met. Children brought up in the UK were often shocked by stories of corporal punishment in other countries and by learning that it was accepted that children had to repeat a year if they didn't attain a certain stan-

Some key points in human rights history

1215   Magna Carta (England)

1688   Bill of Rights (Britain)

1776   Declaration of Independence (USA)

1789   Declaration of the Rights of Man and the Citizen (France)

1833   Abolition of slavery (Britain)

1864   First Geneva Convention (International Red Cross founded)

1899 and 1907

       Hague Conventions (limiting weapons that can be used in war)

1923   Declaration of Geneva

AFTER 1945

1948   Universal Declaration of Human Rights, part of the International Bill of Rights, created in response to the Nazi Holocaust during World War Two

1948   American Declaration of the Rights and Duties of Man

1950   European Convention on Human Rights and Fundamental Freedoms

1951   Convention relating to the status of refugees

1961   International Covenant on Economic, Social and Cultural Rights

International Covenant on Civil and Political Rights
International Convention on the elimination of all forms of racial discrimination

1969   American Convention on Human Rights (Latin America and Caribbean)

1975   Final Act, Helsinki Accords (human rights and confidence-building measures between western and Soviet blocs and neutral countries in Europe)

1979   Convention on the elimination of all forms of discrimination against women

1981   African Charter of Human Rights

1985   Recommendation of the committee of ministers of the Council of Europe on 'Teaching rights and Learning about Human Rights in Schools'

1989   UN Convention on the Rights of the Child

1989   International Labour Organisation convention on indigenous and tribal peoples

1993   World conference on human rights, Vienna Declaration, Plan of Action

1994   UN General Assembly declares 'Decade for Human Rights Education' (1995-2005)

1995   Beijing Declaration and Platform for Action

1998   International Criminal Court

(Taken from Our World, Our Rights, *Amnesty International USA, 2000)*

dard. Listening to children from Kosova and Sierra Leone talk about the rigidity of their former schools led the other children to reflect on their own experience of rights and freedoms.

> *One of the activities we did was a talk show, where we invited other children in the school to be interviewed. They talked about their experiences and lives in schools in other countries. For instance, in Kosova, they only went to school till 11 in the morning because of Albanian schools being outlawed. In these schools there was harsh discipline and no playtimes.* Dave Morris, one of the three Year 5 teachers at Argyle School

Literacy Hour

The Camden Project teachers often used stories as a vehicle for exploring sensitive issues, thus putting a safe distance between the children and the characters so they could explore their own emotions at one remove, and not feel exposed. Issues raised in stories can initiate discussion and encourage children to look beneath the surface of what they see. Stories can also prepare them for coping in difficult situations. When, for example, there has been bullying or aggressive behaviour, a story can create a forum for class discussions which avoids singling out individuals and blaming them.

Similarly, when children use masks and puppets to speak their words in drama and role-plays, they will often talk more freely about difficult matters because the masks give them a degree of anonymity.

The teachers of the younger children in the project recognised literacy hour as a powerful catalyst for looking at rights. Beckford School decided to organise the project differently. Instead of running for one weekly session over a period of ten weeks, which is how the other three schools arranged it, the Beckford teachers decided that it suited them and their Year 1 pupils in this inclusive school, with a large number of children with severe learning difficulties, to compress the project into three consecutive days.

Every morning over the three day period the class teacher read a story to the children. Sometimes they were traditional, well known stories, sometimes they were alternative versions. Then in the afternoon there were a range of exercises to encourage children to interpret the stories, co-taught by James Ware and Tracey Griffiths (see page 22). Key questions would be asked to stimulate children to interpret the story. Children would then make puppets and masks based on different characters in the text and afterwards, in a child-led plenary, a small number would be asked to introduce their characters in role and describe their feelings to the group. This was followed by an adult-led circle time for half an hour, incorporating games and activities to facilitate discussion of the issues raised. The day ended with a review and planning session for the next day.

Sue Emerson offers an account of one of the sessions:

> *After listening to* The Three Little Pigs, *we used memory lines to go over the story after the lunch break and then moved on to collaborative art activities, in the form of puppet and mask-making. Then we moved on to the discussion, which centred on feelings and being able to say sorry. The teachers highlighted the different characteristics of the pigs – shy, lazy, hard-working – and explored with the children alternative endings to the story, like the death of the wolf or saying sorry and reconciliation. They prompted discussion by asking questions such as:*
>
> *What were the different pigs like?*
>
> *How did the pigs feel about leaving home/setting up on their own/being grown-up?*
>
> *How did the wolf feel about being excluded by the pigs?*
>
> *Could the wolf have been misunderstood?*
>
> *What if the wolf had said sorry?*

Literacy and communication skills are important in enabling children to express their feelings, persuade and negotiate with others, critically interpret the media and empower them to stand up for themselves.

All kinds of stories can be used to explore children's rights and citizenship issues using the following structure, employed by schools in the Camden Project.

Structure of story-based session with Key Stage One children
The teacher reads a known text during the morning session as part of the literacy hour.

The children are asked key questions about the behaviour of the characters and their feelings. This incudes the Yes/No strategy and questions to find out more about how the children perceive the relationships within the stories. One way of doing this is to ask them to draw themselves on a post-it and place this drawing somewhere in a picture within the story. Ask them what they can see, hear and how they feel and why. Brainstorm relevant words for feelings.

Activity-based creative learning in small groups:
This might take the form of enacting role-plays using puppets or mask-making or transactional drawings where children are asked to work in groups to draw particular aspects of the story. Teachers can then use these drawings to stimulate discussions.

Plenary:
A number of children volunteer to show and tell what they have been working on to the whole group.

Circle time:
The work is summed up and activities or discussion about the feelings/issues underpinning the stories chosen are analysed. See more about circle time in the section on emotional literacy.

Happiness is........

(Write what happiness means to you)

when my Kittens purr and when I toght them how to walk on two legs.

(Now illustrate your writing)

Emotional literacy as the starting point

Some of the rights translate into 'how does this affect me and the people I'm with?' For instance, the right to association: choosing the friends you want but also thinking about how it feels to be excluded from a friendship group. A key throughout the project was looking at what it means to have a voice, to have rights and how can you have these things and make sure that others have them, too. We worked at these questions through emotional literacy, linking them to the Convention. Lina Fajerman, SC

Although it is a term that is often shrouded in vagueness and inconsistency, in a general sense emotional literacy is about:

- promoting self-esteem and positive identity (see Chapter Four)
- engendering an understanding of one's feelings
- learning to control one's feelings, especially anger, desire, frustration and jealousy
- being able to interpret other people's emotions
- encouraging a sense of empathy
- offering a vocabulary for expressing feelings
- nurturing a sense of cooperation and social responsibility

The parallels and overlaps with some aspects of education for citizenship make them obvious and useful partners. Emotional literacy equips children with the communication skills and self-confidence to express themselves and to function effectively within a group.

For their Key Stage One pupils, Gospel Oak and Beckford Schools saw emotional literacy as the natural vehicle for introducing the subject of human rights.

Giving words and meaning to feelings

James Ware, special needs coordinator and school council teacher who was involved in the project at Beckford School alongside SC's Sue Emerson and Year 1 teacher Tracey Griffiths, explains what they tried to do:

We decided to use emotional literacy as a way of looking at morality in children's stories. I wanted to explore with the children the concept of 'maybe' in moral dilemmas.

Emotional literacy suffused the work that Beckford and Gospel Oak undertook, making it difficult to disassociate it from the other components they included. It informed their thinking and practice in the way they brought rights issues into literacy hour and circle time.

Gospel Oak's reception class teacher, Cindy Warman, shared Beckford's view that emotional literacy had to be the point of departure for looking at rights with young children. Supported by SC's Tina Hyder, she believed that helping children to identify and understand their own feelings and thoughts would lay the foundations for empathic skills, being able to listen to other children and better understand their feelings.

This project was about giving a vocabulary to feelings. It's important that in understanding citizenship, children understand the self. Tina Hyder, SC

A preliminary discussion with the class on the feelings they felt it was important to discuss yielded a consensus that inclusion and exclusion in friendship groups were pressing issues. So Cindy read *The Little Red Hen* and *Lucy's Quarrel*. Children engaged in discussions on how conflicts arise, how they can be resolved and what being a friend was about. The children were asked to consider questions such as:

I don't always like the climbing frame, Mum says no.

Why didn't the animals want to help?
This question helps children analyse and isolate the factors that created the situation.

How do you think this made the hen feel?
Have you ever felt that things weren't fair?
When the hen said the other animals couldn't have any bread, what do you think they felt?
These questions ask children to come to an opinion about what happened.

Why is it important to share?
The children are taken away from the story and encouraged to begin to apply what they have learned to other situations.

How could we change the story so that the hen would share the bread?
Children are invited to come up with strategies to avoid the conflict in the first place.

After they discussed these questions, the pupils considered situations where people had been kind to them and were asked to write about it on a writing frame.

Another method Gospel Oak chose to implement, again rooted in emotional literacy, involved asking pupils about their likes and dislikes in terms of behaviour, their class and the school. Using funds made available through the project, each child was given a disposable camera and asked to take photographs of things they liked and didn't like around the school. Once the photographs were collected, the teacher and children created an encyclopedia of feelings based on the words the children had articulated when describing their photographs, and they illustrated the words with happy or sad or angry faces. When asked to evaluate these sessions,

...many of them said they liked expressing their opinions and being asked what they liked and disliked. They felt that their voices were being valued and that changes could be made to certain things they brought up. In many classrooms you don't get that level of interaction. Tina Hyder, SC

In the end, the class teacher felt that the children, through discussion and activities, had reached an understanding of the necessity of rules and the breadth of rights that they enjoyed.

How useful is emotional literacy in teaching rights?

For young children at Key Stage One, using feelings as a starting point for looking at the concept of rights and responsibilities is not only valid but necessary.

The power of emotional literacy to engage children in citizenship issues can't be overestimated. As Don Rowe puts it in *Introducing Citizenship: A Handbook for Primary Schools*:

Thinking informs and to some extent controls the emotions, but feelings motivate us to care or not to care, to be involved or to withdraw. Both [thinking and feeling] strongly influence our actions, the latter in turn shaping and developing how we think and feel. Citizenship education is a prime curriculum location for the promotion of emotional as well as moral and political literacy.

Magic circles

Circle time is a valuable vehicle for reinforcing issues that have come up in the lesson and is already a regular fixture in primary school schedules, usually on a weekly basis.

Although there are many variations, it is generally a time when children come together in a circle to discuss topics and issues. A set of simple rules – only one person speaks at a time, no interruptions, taking account of others' feelings – renders it a time when pupils can develop social skills in a secure and affirming environment. Circle time is space in which children can express their opinions openly, have their views listened to and learn to listen to others. Because of this, it's an ideal time for resolving conflicts, making decisions that affect the whole class and dealing with difficult issues or news that children have found distressing or worthy of comment.

Lorna Farrington, one of Britain's foremost exponents of circle time, explains its special quality as experienced at the Plymouth primary school where she was headteacher:

> *Everyone learns that what they have to say is valid, valuable and valued by the others in the class or group – even if their wish is simply to say 'pass' when it's their turn in the circle. Children were learning that they had the right to have a say, but not the right to be right.*

At Beckford, teachers would take the story read that morning and use it as a point of departure for discussing a particular issue. For instance, when *Cinderella* was the story that they had explored in the morning, the teachers would kick off circle time in the afternoon by asking the children how, for example, they would feel in her position and then open the discussion out to talk about fairness and equality.

Choosing a more sophisticated text with its Year 3 pupils, Torriano Juniors used the snake story to help children understand the differences between aggression and assertiveness. The story shows that it is an easy transition from being angry aggressor to victim, and that neither is desirable.

A variation of the following activity was used by some of the schools to help children focus on their own feelings and the

THE SNAKE STORY

A very wicked snake infested a road and bit everyone who walked by. A holy man was passing on the road and the snake rushed at him to bite him. The holy man looked at the snake and said quite calmly: 'You want to bite me, don't you? Well, go ahead.'

The snake was shocked by this strange response and overwhelmed by the gentleness of the holy man. The man said: 'Listen to me, dear friend. Could you promise me that you won't bite anyone from now on?' The snake bowed to the holy man and agreed. The man went on his way and the snake began his new life of non-violence.

Soon everyone in the neighbourhood discovered that the snake was harmless and the young boys began to tease him mercilessly. They dragged him around by his tail and threw stones at him. But the snake kept his promise to the holy man.

Fortunately, the holy man came by to see the snake and was shocked to see him so battered and bruised. He asked the snake what had happened and the snake said: 'You said I should not bite anyone. But people are so very cruel.'

The holy man said: 'I asked you not to bite anyone. But I didn't tell you not to hiss!' (from Cattanach, 1994)

feelings of others and to equip them with some of the vocabulary needed to express their feelings.

Pupil activity: Developing emotional vocabulary

Working in pairs, one child takes photographs of the other expressing a number of different facial expressions. They are asked to show what it looks like when we are angry/sad/happy/scared/surprised/excited/cheeky, etc. They are then asked to describe the situations when they have these feelings. This can move on to an exploration of feelings that are more difficult to understand, such as guilt, jealousy, irritation and frustration. The class reviews their observations in circle time and they discuss why it is important to know how we feel and how we can tell how other people are feeling. Afterwards, the photos are all collected in a class book and labelled with the matching emotions.

Self-evaluation

After each piece of project work or group activity, pupils can be asked to evaluate their performance, not only in terms of the knowledge and understanding they have gained but also of the way they worked and cooperated with others in their group. This encourages them to take greater responsibility for their own learning and to reflect on their interactions. It may also help them to understand the supportive role that evaluation can play, rather than seeing it as criticism on the part of the teacher.

Pupil Activity: Evaluating my work

Teachers may want to offer these guidelines to pupils when it comes to doing self-evaluations.

Did I listen to other people's ideas?

Did I show other people that I was listening to them?

Did I ask questions?

Did I explain why I agreed or disagreed with other people?

Was I fully involved in class discussions?
(Adapted from Harding and Unwin, 1998)

Evaluation doesn't have to be a tedious process. There are ways of bringing an element of fun into comments and judgments. Some of the Camden schools used cut-out faces at the end of each session, which helped to indicate to teachers what their pupils thought about their lessons. The Yes/No technique could be combined with the questions above in evaluations.

Making time to hear what children enjoy and what they don't like and why is very useful feedback. But more than this, a dialogue is created between teacher and children, where children's views are important and can make a difference. It makes for an interesting shift in classroom dynamics. Cindy Warman, Gospel Oak School

Confidentiality

Teachers must be prepared to deal with a range of issues that children might raise. The Camden teachers found that it was sometimes necessary to follow up sensitive matters that children had talked about in class with one to one sessions. The PSHE and Citizenship guidance offers some advice on how to handle disclosures. It suggests first of all that there should be a school policy on confidentiality so that all staff members respond to an agreed procedure. If children talk about activities that are illegal, teachers are not necessarily required to inform the police. But if they receive information about behaviour likely to cause harm to the child or to others, they must pass it on to the appropriate agency and inform the child that they are doing so.

Similarly, teachers are not obliged to pass on information about pupils to their parents, although where they are at moral or physical risk they must ensure that the pupil is aware of the risks. In lessons, teachers should establish from the beginning that it is inappropriate to disclose certain personal information. Pupils need to be clear about not putting pressure on one another to answer questions about their personal lives. All children have the right to privacy and all child welfare organisations work within agreed guidelines for protecting children's private lives.

In many of the ways demonstrated here – and through many others within teachers' individual experiences – children in primary schools can be helped to develop their self-confidence and sense of worth. This supports their rights to their own identity and to playing an active, confident part in the society to which they belong – in their classroom, in the school as a whole and beyond the school gates – no matter what their age.

Using drama

Drama is part of the curriculum and extends language and literacy skills. As a form of participation, drama challenges children to draw on their powers of emotional and social expression in a collaborative creative act. It's a learning method that by definition develops pupils' rights to freedom of expression.

Of the many varieties of classroom dramatic activity available to teachers, role-plays and simulations give scope for identifying with the needs of other children or adults in different places, times and situations. You can set up a Victorian classroom or make decisions about building a motorway or dramatise different endings to books you read in literacy hour. You can, as some schools have done, create Anglo Saxon hearings or explore the dynamics of village life in India through putting items to be decided to an elected *panchayat* or village council.

Drama works best when the right degrees of authentic context and free imaginative expression are matched. In other words, too much factual input can kill off the spontaneity of dramatic participation, whereas too much invention takes the learning away from the realms of reality.

Role-plays and simulations can also be used directly for politicised learning about elections and parliaments. Dramatic theory is best learned at secondary levels, but primary children are well able to take part in mock elections and mock parliamentary sessions on issues of topical concern. Such activities can extend the benefits that children gain from being part of a school council or children's parliament, bringing a wider national or global context into the classroom (see PART THREE on learning for global citizenship).

The teacher in role
Teachers might think of themselves taking on the role of the Speaker of the House, appreciating children's comments and feeding their views back, rather than asserting their own ideas. In discussions where the objective is to encourage the views of the children, teachers need to weigh up the pros and cons of the different roles they can adopt:

- The teacher may be an impartial chairperson

- S/he may state a personal viewpoint

- S/he may present children with a wide range of alternatives and ensure that all sides are brought forward

- S/he can play devil's advocate, consciously taking up the opposite position to the one expressed by the children. (This needs to be explained in advance to the class.)

Each situation needs to be assessed according to the needs of the pupils and what they objectives of the session are.

The diagram below shows how teachers can assume a number of different roles:

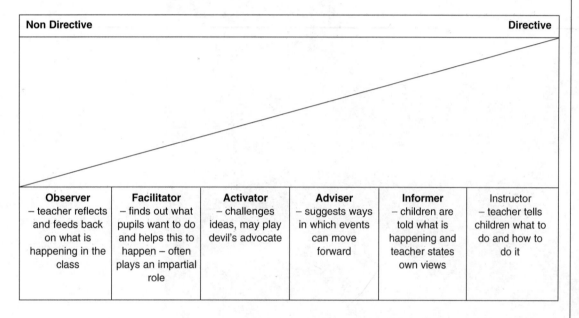

Non Directive					Directive
Observer – teacher reflects and feeds back on what is happening in the class	**Facilitator** – finds out what pupils want to do and helps this to happen – often plays an impartial role	**Activator** – challenges ideas, may play devil's advocate	**Adviser** – suggests ways in which events can move forward	**Informer** – children are told what is happening and teacher states own views	Instructor – teacher tells children what to do and how to do it

Drama and art in various forms were drawn on by all the schools to illustrate and express different aspects of children's rights.

At Gospel Oak, Cindy Harman led her class in an exploration of conflict resolution through story and drama. First she read *Lucy's Quarrel*. Then she presented two dolls having an argument and asked the children to search for ways to resolve it. The dolls were Persona Dolls, specially designed to be used by teachers to raise issues around prejudice and differentness.

After they read *The Little Red Hen*, pupils were asked to paint pictures on the theme of being kind. That led to a re-reading of the story. The children then made masks, after which they acted out the story with different endings, wearing the masks they had made.

> *We worked from the hypothesis that once children understood their own feelings better, they would understand each other better. So we gave them the building blocks for empathy by designing activities that would allow them to identify their own feelings and thoughts. This led to them being able to listen better to others and, ultimately, to come to some consensus about issues around them.* Tina Hyder, SC

Learning from mistakes

Beckford's use of puppets and masks to act out themes raised in the stories earlier in the day was not, in the eyes of SENCO coordinator James Ware, an unqualified success. As such, it offers a cautionary tale to teachers about designing projects to fit the age group and laying foundations for work that the children may be unaccustomed to.

There are two possible explanations for what James saw as the weakness of integrating masks and puppets into role-play scenarios. The first one is that some children under the age of

seven may have difficulties entering into the feelings and motivations of others, which can mean that role-play is not going to have the impact that it will have with older children. The other reason could be that, as James suggested, the children were unfamiliar with working with puppets and masks. He felt the activity lacked depth, despite the fact that the children loved the experience.

We needed to be more focused and to have more time to plan and execute the project as well as to evaluate it. I expected too much of the children's understanding and their ability to work with puppets. They may not have been familiar to them, given the many cultures our pupils come from. So it wasn't a success but I learned a lot. I believe we use talking too much in classrooms. This kind of working (using art and drama) used to happen in schools much more as a matter of course. But there's no reason why they can't be used today when they fit into the key skills of the national curriculum, which they did in this project. James Ware, teacher at Beckford School

Even so, masks gave children the illusion of protectiveness in the plenaries. Some of them made whispered disclosures to their class teacher about people hurting them at home or keeping bad secrets.

With older children, there is more scope for sophisticated drama activities. Drama has the power to cut to the heart of an issue, even quite a personal one, but to do so one step removed so that children don't feel intimidated and are more willing to engage with it. It also allows children the freedom to deal with issues they wish to air in a creative way that is easily shared with others.

While taking a more conventionally cognitive approach than any of the other three schools in the project, Argyle School used drama to good advantage when disseminating the lessons the Year 5 children had learned, in an assembly to the rest of the school.

We used drama to convey the main philosophies of what we were doing. For example, we presented a playground scenario where an older boy barges past a younger child. The younger child, a girl, challenges him assertively, not aggressively, by saying 'I don't like what you did.' Another scenario involved a child finding a book bag in the playground. It exposed the moral dilemma that flickers through children's minds: should I have a look inside and see if there's something interesting in it? Dave Morris, teacher at Argyle School

Chapter Three

LIVING RIGHTS:
Methodology

Save the Children and sister organisations working in the field of children's rights advocate the view that learning *about* citizenship isn't enough. Being taught the facts without being given opportunities to experience the concept is no different to what has been called citizenship or civics in the past: preparing the citizens of the future to vote and become part of the democratic process. SC is committed to giving children the opportunity to learn *through* citizenship as well; enabling pupils to see their roles as active citizens now and become involved in making decisions and debating ideas, feeling confident in the belief that they have something to contribute today.

Rights and issues around the democratic process are already in the ether of all schools, and not just in the curriculum. They are what fuels school councils, they are recurring themes in circle time, they are there for the taking in the morality of stories that are read in literacy hour – whether in fantasy stories like *Cinderella* or in stories rooted in reality like *Journey to Jo'burg* – and in history and geography studies.

Like all sound pedagogic practice, rights education involves both cognitive and experiential learning: about teaching the facts, the concepts and events that are relevant *and* about giving children the experience to learn it actively. By definition it must involve children exercising their rights as part of the learning process; giving them the opportunity to learn on their own terms in ways that they have asked for it to be delivered – within reason. It must involve both school ethos and classroom management based on the values of justice and democracy.

The Camden teachers had diverse experiences of creating an experiential learning environment for rights education. For some it was easier than for others. But all felt that it had given them something invaluable that would inform their teaching and thinking forevermore.

The inset session that Save the Children ran for the project teachers concentrated on the implications of using different teaching styles and techniques to encourage children's participation. Although the curriculum and time constraints were seen as major barriers, the teachers nevertheless recognised the importance of creating a climate in the classroom in which children felt self-assured, comfortable and confident enough to take part.

A *risky business*

As well as using strategies such as circle time and group work, the teachers also acknowledged the importance of their own attitudes and expectations of the children. They had to believe in the children if the children were to believe in themselves, and this could only happen if the teachers were prepared to take risks. It meant them loosening some of their control and allowing children to take the lead sometimes. As unnerving as this was for some of the teachers, it emerged time and again that children had the capacity, maturity and willingness to make sensible decisions.

To allow this to happen, the teachers needed to create opportunities where children could be genuinely consulted, have their views acted upon and where they could critically assess and question the status quo. This was challenging for teachers in both positive and negative ways. It questioned the authority of the teachers – never a comfortable proposition – but it also led, the

Now I feel how it is going and have a feel for the mood of the class, I adapt and change things as needed...there is not a rigid structure. They have been telling me what they want to do and how they want to do it and so there is a more enjoyable lesson.

Children can find being given more responsibility quite scary.

Despite detailed pre-planning, we had to leave space to react to how the children were feeling on any given day and this sometimes meant that it was necessary to shorten or omit parts of the session.

It's really interesting when they tell you what they think.

The most successful activity was when children were able to take their own photographs of activities and areas of the school they like and don't like using disposable cameras.

teachers found, to increased mutual trust, a willingness on the part of children to accept more responsibility for the welfare of others and an enhanced sense of confidence that the teachers felt in their pupils, as reflected in these quotations.

When encouraging children to participate, adults often have to challenge not only their existing practice but also the hierarchies that exist in schools. For participation to be genuine, power has to be given to children. But to what extent is this possible? And to what extent are adults able to respond to children's expressed needs and concerns, particularly when they challenge institutional practices and, at times, the teachers' authority and responsibility? To what extent, finally, can teachers allow children power when they have not only legal responsibilities towards them but also the obligation to provide for and protect them as laid out in the Convention on the Rights of the Child?

These questions need to be looked at from the opposite side of the fence, too: if children are not given the opportunities to contribute to and practise decision-making, particularly in matters which directly affect them, how will they ever learn to take responsibility for themselves? And ultimately, how can their rights be respected?

Participation in more than name

Being clear about the concept of participation is important for teachers. Are children truly participating when they are asked for their opinions on a subject which is predetermined by adults or when little notice is taken of what they say when they are supposedly given a voice? When participation is in name only, children sense it and come to believe that it is a meaningless concept.

If, however, they are involved in a school council where they understand the limitations of their decision-making power but

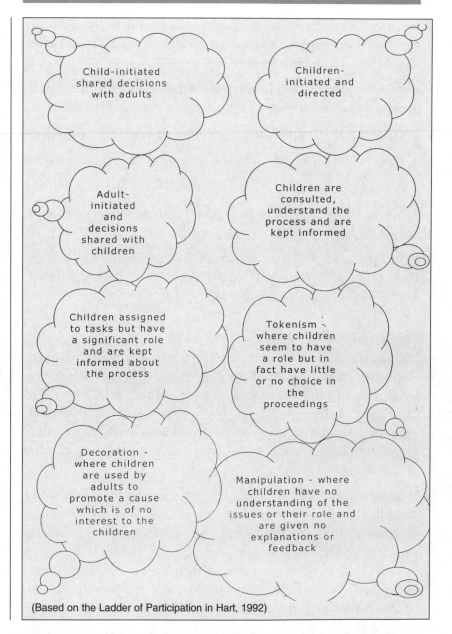

Child-initiated shared decisions with adults

Children-initiated and directed

Adult-initiated and decisions shared with children

Children are consulted, understand the process and are kept informed

Children assigned to tasks but have a significant role and are kept informed about the process

Tokenism - where children seem to have a role but in fact have little or no choice in the proceedings

Decoration - where children are used by adults to promote a cause which is of no interest to the children

Manipulation - where children have no understanding of the issues or their role and are given no explanations or feedback

(Based on the Ladder of Participation in Hart, 1992)

find their views being taken into serious consideration nonetheless, they will see participation as a useful exercise and themselves as having a valued role to play.

According to Hart (1992), there are requirements that need to be in place before an activity can be deemed to be truly participative:

- the intention of the project should be made clear to children

- they should understand how decisions are going to be made

- their role should be meaningful rather than decorative

- their involvement must be voluntary and based on knowledge of the project

Hart's levels of participation (originally presented as a stepladder leading upwards towards full participation) are more fully represented in the diagram on page 33.

Loosening the reins

It's easy for teachers to set the agenda unnecessarily instead of encouraging pupils to take the initiative in deciding, for instance, what shape a project will take. But it's not that difficult to shed that habit. Before embarking on a piece of work or project, children could be drawn in to make decisions or at least air their views about what they would like to get out of it and what direction might be taken to achieve their aims.

In the Camden project, some teachers were initially reticent about sharing their power. Trained to be well prepared, organised and in control of their classrooms, their ambivalence was wholly understandable. But as they involved the children more and become increasingly responsive to their needs, they found their classrooms became more harmonious. For their part, they acquired better insights into their pupils' experiences and feelings.

TEACHERS' ACTIVITY

This activity will help teachers in their understanding of the concept of participation:

Look at the types of participation shown below and discuss which fit with the different kinds of participation outlined in Hart's levels on the previous page. There are no right and wrong answers.

Pre-school children are given political placards by adults to carry in a demonstration.

Children develop their own version of cricket to suit their situation with their own rules.

Children are asked to design their ideal playground. Adults synthesise the results and come up with a 'children's design.'

Children are given t-shirts related to a cause that they have little understanding of.

Adults choose some children to speak as part of a conference panel.

Children's views are solicited by a group of adults in a project and are treated seriously.

Children are asked to design, publish and distribute their own school or community newsletter.

Expectations were raised, motivation and enthusiasm grew and aspects of children's personal and emotional development were enriched.

You have to get a feeling of what the kids know and what's important in their lives rather than deciding what they're ready for. After the project, we did lots of basic activities on health and drugs. I did it following their lead. They really wanted to know more about it after declaring one of their rights to be 'all children should be safe from drugs'.

If I were to do it with my class now, they'd have new ideas and I'd have to look at it from a different angle because they're different children and a different age group. We could do work on the police, going on protests – there's so much you can do on rights. Nastasha Ewing, teacher at Torriano Juniors.

Although Natasha, as a recently qualified teacher, was nervous about taking risks – which is in essence what taking children's lead involves – she and her SC worker Lina Fajerman developed a way of working that involved children having the opportunity to say what they'd like to do in the next session. What they said, more or less unanimously, was that they wanted stories, drama and art. So stories and drama and art were the routes through which they learned about rights.

Natasha developed the idea of a body made of cardboard with children writing on it what they believed to be their rights. We collected their writings, some of which SC later produced as posters: things like 'we have the right to live in a nice place' and 'I have the right to make up my own mind.' Lina Fajerman, SC.

At Gospel Oak, not only were the children given cameras to photograph their likes and dislikes, but they were asked to do an evaluation after each session. For children in reception class to feel that their ideas and views are important is a rare but empowering experience.

You don't find that level of interaction in many classrooms. It was so important for the project and for the children themselves that they were asked their opinions throughout the process and that they knew that their voices were being valued. They learned that there was a link between feelings and rights and the class teacher, Cindy, learned that she could make changes to her teaching based on the children's evaluation of each session. Tina Hyder, SC

Argyle used a dilemma game devised by the teachers and SC's Bharti Mepani to stimulate discussion among the participating Year 5 pupils. The teachers would read out a statement like 'children should be given regular homework' or 'children of your age should go to bed at nine' or 'you should always do what an adult tells you' and pupils would have to say whether they agree, strongly agree, disagree or strongly disagree. As well as serving as a catalyst for debate, it helped illustrate to the children how issues are rarely black and white. They also helped decide what subjects would come up for discussion in future sessions.

We had a comment box where children could put in ideas that would be dealt with in class and which led to further discussions about things like being excluded from friendship groups. They put in a variety of things, from 'I don't like when people call me names' to 'we should have a better school menu.' Dave Morris, Argyle

An activity generated by the project was the development of a school charter.

The children had the idea of finding out what existed in other schools. So we developed a questionnaire featuring questions like 'do you have homework?' and 'how are you punished in school?' and 'what's the food like?' and distributed them to other primary schools in the area. Dave Morris, Argyle

Because the oldest children in the project were from Argyle, its teachers and SC worker were able to introduce more challenging methodologies borne of more sophisticated thinking. As Dave Morris put it:

It was clear to us that children had to develop their own awareness of where they fit in. This project allowed them to think in terms of the effect they can have on their immediate community, of the cause and effect of their actions and of doing something positive in their environment to reverse the trend of self-centredness that all children are subject to.

The project culminated in the Year 5 classes' participation in Footsteps for Peace, a yearly tradition in Japan in which a Peace Bus travels to other countries around the world greeting school-children and collecting footsteps on which messages are written. In preparation for the arrival of the bus in England, the Year 5 children, teachers and SC worker galvanised everyone in the school to write down on a giant footstep one thing they would like to change in the world, and this was presented to the Peace Bus. The footstep and many others like it from all over the world eventually ended up at the European Court of Human Rights in the Hague.

Skills and strategies for participation

For children to exercise their rights, they need to be equipped with the skills to participate. They need:

to be able to make their opinions clear
to state their needs
practice in decision making
to be able to listen
to feel empathy

They also need to have their views listened to and taken into account and to have the validity of the emotions they express accepted.

Summary of basic communication skills fundamental to citizenship education

Key Stage 1	Key Stage 2
	Assessing different points of view
Listening to others	Detecting bias, opinion, stereotypes
Asking questions	
Expressing a view	Presenting an argument
Stating an opinion	Finding and selecting evidence
Resolving arguments	Negotiating
Being willing to change one's mind	Arguing effectively
	Basing arguments on evidence
	Accepting differences of opinion

Discussion and debate

It is vital that children be encouraged to express their opinions freely and fluently. But it's equally important that their opinions are informed. It's not always easy for children to give their own opinions rather than their friends' or those they think their teacher wants to hear. Creating a climate of trust, security and mutual respect, where children can feel confident that any personal opinions they express will be listened to and acknowledged, is essential. If children become used to having their views valued, they will become more confident.

There are many ways of promoting discussion in the classroom. They range from formalised debates with designated speakers arguing for or against a topic to simulated meetings of communities or town councils (see the role-play section below). All fit into the speaking and listening requirements of the national curriculum.

Work in small groups can be effective preparation for whole class discussion, allowing even shy children to rehearse their ideas and delivery. Group work can be constructed as collaborative tasks such as sorting pictures, matching captions or ranking sets of opinions in priority order. Recognition and encouragement should be given for the achievement of good group communication.

The following activity is helpful for developing discussion skills and verbal expression of ideas.

PUPIL ACTIVITY: THE YES/NO INTERLUDE

This is a simple technique for encouraging discussion of contentious issues. Designate two opposite corners of the room YES and NO. Read out a statement and ask children to position themselves along a line between the two corners according to how strongly they agree or disagree with the statement. Camden teachers used this technique after reading stories such as *Cinderella*, asking questions like 'was it fair that Cinderella did all the work?' and 'should she have gone to the ball?' These led to broader discussions about name-calling, exclusion and being treated fairly.

Examples of statements you might use:

– All children must wear school uniforms

– If children disagree with adults, they should be able to say so

– Children should have a say in what the school teaches and whether there is homework

– Children should give their teachers feedback on their performance

Debate is an important part of citizenship education. Disagreements between young children, however, are short on debating skills and long on hot tempers. Annabelle Dixon argues that although this isn't surprising, it can be avoided if children are equipped with two things: they are clear about what the ground rules are and they know what language is required.

Genuine participation can be time-consuming. A quick way to 'consult' may be to outline what is intended and ask if there are any objections. Chances are there will be total silence. An alternative is to get children to discuss the issue in pairs, which gives them the chance to consider the question and means they don't have to stick their necks out so much in discussion.

Making Decisions

Children can be involved in decisions about classroom organisation. They could decide, for instance, between having a nature table or a sand table. This can be done by consensus or by voting, through collaborative and cooperative group work or as individuals. Decisions that affect the whole class can be made by taking a vote and letting the majority decide. It's important to ask the minority how they feel about this and to find out from the majority group how they think the views of the minority might be accommodated. Children will know already that decisions often don't satisfy everyone, but that sometimes there are ways for the views of minorities to be taken on board. The ideas of compromise, consensus negotiation and vetoes can be introduced and practised.

The fact that children's views are sought and that they are trusted with making decisions conveys to them the affirming and supportive message that what they think matters.

As Annabelle Dixon puts it:

> *...it is the provision of opportunities to take decisions that will probably provide the most influential experiences. This has an impact on children's sense of self-esteem, on the feeling that they can take responsibility for themselves and be in control, thereby helping to counteract the culture of what American researchers refer to as 'learned helplessness.'*

PUPILS' ACTIVITY: THE TWO DONKEYS – A LESSON IN COOPERATION

You will need rope or long scarves, something nice to eat that can be shared in two bowls, like raisins, and copies of the donkey story cartoon cut up into strips.

What to do:

- Ask for two volunteers. You can put donkey ears on them to give them 'authenticity.'

- Explain to the group that you are worried the donkeys will stray so you are going to tie them together.

- Tie the two children together around the waist back to back with several feet of rope/scarf connecting them.

- Stand the donkeys back to back and show each of them the bowls of food on opposite sides of the room but out of reach.

- A tug of war will soon develop.

- Before the stronger child reaches the food, stop the tug of war and ask the group how they can ensure that both donkeys get the food.

- Take suggestions from the group and continue until someone suggests a solution as follows:

  Let the donkeys go to one side of the room together to collect the food and then go to the other side.

- Share the two bowls of food with the whole group.

- Show the group the picture and take them through the story again.

(This idea originates from Quaker Peace and Service)

This picture, based on an original design by the League of Nations, is reproduced with kind permission from Quaker Peace and Service and Social Witness.

The next activity is of a general nature for thinking about rights and learning what the UN Convention on the Rights of the Child contains. It can be used with the summaries of the Convention on page 7 to relate children's own ideas about their rights to what has been agreed by the international community.

PUPIL ACTIVITY: DEVELOPING A CLASS CHARTER

Prepare a number of cards and write along the top 'Children should have the right to...'

Individually, pupils should complete the sentence and then, in small groups, discuss what they have written. Then all the children come together in a circle and discuss which rights should be in their class charter. They should be directed to choosing rights that apply to everyone in the class. (Brownlie, 1998)

THE CHILDREN'S PARLIAMENT

This is a government sponsored project that allows children to be involved in democratic processes at national level. They take part in mock debates and are able to meet with and grill ministers at the House of Commons.

To summarise, a course on children's rights for citizenship will have a content component as well as an experiential one. Content, as suggested in the first part of this book, involves direct learning about international instruments such as the UN Convention on the Rights of the Child. The experiential element can take different forms but will exemplify specific children's rights, such as freedom of expression, freedom of association and peaceful assembly.

The extent to which pupils are able to participate in their own learning processes is a good indicator of how rights-focused the learning methods are.

Chapter Four

SELF-ESTEEM AND CHILDREN'S RIGHTS

The curriculum that is taught in schools needs to incorporate each individual child's background, to give them self-worth and pride in who they are. Doreen Lawrence (in Richardson and Wood, 2000)

Self-esteem is one of the components of emotional intelligence. It's being dealt with separately here to underline its centrality in all work on the issue of rights and citizenship.

Sigmund Freud referred to the establishment of self-esteem and a sense of self-worth as the 'golden seed,' upon which the future development and happiness of the individual is based.

The ability to value oneself and others and to establish and negotiate relationships are essential building blocks of rights and citizenship education. Self-esteem is what enables children to fulfil their potential and to develop the skills they need to be effective citizens.

The teachers in the Camden project appreciated the importance of self-esteem in helping children develop a sense of their own worth and potential as individuals. This includes feeling pride in their cultural background and having the ability to cope with new situations and challenges.

It entails a greater understanding of feelings and the need for children, from the earliest age, to develop the skills they need to identify and negotiate their rights and entitlements within friendships, the classroom and the wider world.

There is a increasing body of research and evidence to point to self-esteem having a crucial role to play in raising children's academic achievement and motivation as well as in enhancing their personal and social skills.

Pickering's six reasons why children's voices and involvement are essential to school improvement (1997) all implicitly point to the necessity for positive self-esteem and for schools to work to address its development.

1. Pupils need to be at the centre of their learning in order to increase motivation and educational productivity.

2. Pupils are valuable for the feedback they can give about their learning.

3. Pupils need to be included in the debate about their learning because it is *their* learning.

4. Pupils can be powerful partners in school improvement as co-researchers.

5. Pupils should be involved in responsible debate about their education, because this reflects the level of responsibility that many have in their lives outside of school.

6. Schools must work with and reflect the pupils' world.

Self-esteem helps to imbue children with the confidence they need to succeed and means they are more readily disposed to consider someone else's point of view and to stand up for it. Studies have shown that children with high self-regard are less likely to tolerate discrimination and inequality and more likely to take a stand against injustice. On the other hand, poor self-image has been cited as a source of interpersonal conflict. If children can understand and name their feelings, they are less likely to become frustrated and aggressive.

Those with a well-developed and positive image of themselves have the ability to be self-critical and to realistically assess their own strengths and weaknesses. They are able to recognise the worth of others and to be encouraging and supportive. They can accept criticism without becoming overly defensive; work well in a group without needing to dominate or impose their own ideas; and be able to deal with conflict without resorting to physical and verbal aggression. (Fountain, 1990)

Self-esteem and rights

Article 29 of the UN Convention on the Rights of the child states that:

the education of the child shall be directed to the development of the child's personality, talents and mental and physical abilities to their fullest potential (and to) the preparation of the child for responsible life in a free society.

The fostering of self-esteem is key in ensuring this article is met, both in terms of children fulfilling their true potential for education and happiness and also of their willingness to recognise the rights of others and take action, where necessary, on their behalf. The framework for PSHE and Citizenship Education acknowledges the importance of this when it states: '*...pupils should be taught... to feel positive about themselves (for example by having their achievements recognised and by being given positive feedback about themselves)*'.

Chapter Five

GETTING THE WHOLE SCHOOL ON BOARD

What makes a school's ethos	
Underpinning values	**Relationships**
trust	pupil-pupil
honesty	pupil-adult
equality	adult-adult
justice	management
Student participation	**Policies and standards**
school councils	mission statements
clubs	citizenship policies
extra-curricular	equal opportunities
community activities	anti-bullying behaviour
	playground policy
Learning environment	
	Participation of whole
physical	school community
emotional	(regular visitors)

Based on Development Education Association, 1999 (2)

Schools are the matrix of freedom, not just by what they teach but also by what they do. Chief Rabbi Jonathan Sacks, Times Educational Supplement, June 18 1999

Aspects of the whole school ethos

So far this book has focused on classroom activities. This chapter explores how a rights approach can be broadened out to the whole school, its ethos and policies – particularly concerning behaviour – and to school councils, staff, management and governors. It will also look at how the school relates to parents and the wider community.

The whole school ethos encompasses everything that happens in the school and can be summed up in the diagram on the left.

Schools are communities which can and should be an example of respect for the individual and for difference, for tolerance and for equality of opportunity. (Council of Europe, 1985)

The Camden Project teachers were working towards a whole school ethos where:

– everyone, particularly children, participates more

– children take greater responsibility for their own learning

– school councils are important and valued vehicles for children's views and opinions

– children's views are taken seriously

– children are involved in developing school policies

– children fulfil their role as responsible members of the school community

Whether they succeeded or not will be discussed later in this chapter.

Lorna Farrington, speaking from her experience as a headteacher in a Plymouth primary school, describes the process of involving all children in the school community:

I didn't come here to impose my philosophy on the school. It was the school that engendered a philosophical response that works. Everything that we have done has been informed by what staff and children have to say. (Farrington, 1997)

Acknowledging children's rights

One cannot teach about democracy and rights in an environment that is undemocratic and where children's rights are not acknowledged. The draft guidance on PSHE and Citizenship (2000) points out that what is taught and learned in PSHE and Citizenship can be reinforced or, conversely, undermined by whether or not it is consistent with the school's values and ethos.

The guidance suggests:

• establishing a common sense of purpose and respecting difference

• having a shared and practised mission statement

• creating a welcoming atmosphere

• establishing codes of conduct for encouraging positive behaviour and relationships

• challenging discrimination and bullying

• promoting courtesy and respect

• raising and recognising achievement

• consulting and valuing staff and pupils as individuals

• sharing ideals and concerns

• caring for each other, the community and the environment

While the teachers in the Camden Project all worked in schools with a positive, child-centred ethos and felt they succeeded in fulfiling the aims above with their own classes, some felt that they had not succeeded in disseminating their experience and practice of establishing a rights-based approach to the school as a whole or to parents because of time and organisational constraints and, it must be said, disinterest.

At Torriano Juniors, teacher Natasha Ewing, working alongside SC's Lina Fajerman, arguably made the most headway of all the teachers in the project of getting the ideas spread beyond her classroom. She organised her class to present a juniors assembly on children's rights to the rest of the school, in which the children acted in a number of short role-plays to illustrate specific rights.

We wanted this project to be a paradigm for a whole school approach. That's why it was deliberately spread across different age groups in the four schools. Lina Fajerman, SC

Natasha produced her own materials, alongside some devised by Lina, to use with her class and to share with colleagues. Among them were cards with scenarios for the children to act out in role-plays, lists of rights that pupils were asked to prioritise and the UN Convention that Lina rewrote for seven year olds. Thanks to the assembly that Natasha's class presented on their work on rights, some of her colleagues decided to take up the rights theme themselves and have used Natasha's home-made resources.

But their plan to do a presentation for parents as a culmination of the ten week project was cancelled and ultimately dropped because curriculum issues took priority. In the end, Natasha and Lina produced certificates for each child to be presented with and to take home – where, it was hoped, they would discuss with parents what the project was about.

At Gospel Oak, attempts were also made to engage the rest of the school, but to no avail.

> *It was very hard to make an impact on the rest of the school. Cindy and I tried to speak to staff and governors at meetings but it didn't come through. Given the difficult circumstances at the school at the time, I doubt that very much of what we did was sustained. But I think it changed the way Cindy has interacted with children ever since. The idea that young children could contribute and help impact on her planning was new for her.* Tina Hyder, SC

Children at Argyle School had the idea of doing a talk show, to which they invited other children in the school to come and speak about their experiences in schools in other countries. Dave Morris and SC's Bharti Mepani also involved the rest of the school in getting involved in Footsteps for Peace. The Year 5s had an assembly as well, where the children used drama to convey the main philosophies of the project to the rest of the school.

Resources for the whole school were put together by the then head of PSHE, based on the work the teachers had done during the ten weeks. Since she left the school, the impetus to carry on the work has gone.

PLANNING A WHOLE SCHOOL APPROACH

As all teachers and parents will know from their own experience, children are sensitive to injustice, hypocrisy and inconsistencies. The QCA guidelines for PSHE and Education for Citizenship acknowledge the problems that might occur when schools teach rights education but use behaviour management practices, for instance, that fly in the face of children's rights. The guidelines, for that reason, stress the importance of ensuring that the values of citizenship and rights education are reflected in the way the school is managed and run:

> *Research shows that pupils can be keenly aware of discrepancies between values stated and values practised and that such inconsistencies can lead to scepticism about the values stated.*

The guidelines list three learning strategies that allow for a holistic delivery of rights education:

- a *skills* approach, with decision-making, working with others, etc as a starting point

- an *opportunities* approach, using topical issues as a stimulus for debates, public performances and other school activities

- a *thematic* approach, where themes such as rights, responsibilities and democracy are used to develop children's knowledge, understanding, skills and attitudes.

One of the aims of the Camden Project was to disseminate the innovative practice that emerged from it to the rest of the school community so that models could be developed and sustained. This, by and large, did not happen for a variety of reasons associated with citizenship being low on the priority list of most schools.

But all the teachers involved in the project appreciated the importance of the three QCA guidelines and sought ways to take a holistic, all-embracing approach to them. What became clear from their experiences was that, although a rights approach required new thinking and strategies, there was plenty of good practice already in existence that they could adapt for their own use.

In the planning stage, they took an audit of what was already happening in their schools and what resources were available. They mapped out all the current practice on rights and then identified aspects that could be further developed and expanded as well as any gaps, including training and resource needs.

School Policies

A school adopting a rights approach should make that fact explicit to everyone concerned with the school. In addition, developing school policies means that the involvement of the school's 'stakeholders' – parents, non-teaching staff and local community members – is essential. Such policies are a manifestation of the school's commitment to its principles and provide a reference point for pupils, staff and parents. They can be one important way in which the school communicates a consistent message about itself to parents and the wider community.

A rights agenda provides a rational framework for equal opportunities policies. Helping children to recognise that bullying, racism, sexism, etc are violations of their rights will help them to understand that rights are universal and not just for poor, oppressed people in far-off places. They can begin to understand that there are common values that transcend cultural differences and which place obligations on us all. Just knowing that these rights exist can provide support and security for children whose rights are being abused and will hopefully empower them to come forward in the knowledge that action will be taken on their behalf.

> *Citizenship education should not just be about teaching children to be good citizens when they grow up; it's also about their rights to be listened to and taken seriously. It needs to be in the curriculum, but also embedded in democratic structures in schools.* Lansdown, 1998.

School policies need to encompass classroom assistants, kitchen staff, dinner and playground supervisors, caretakers and school-keepers, all of whom have an impact on pupils.

While having policies is important, they will only have validity and credibility if they are implemented. Look at the rules of the school: is there one set for children and another for teachers and other adults? Children should have clear instructions on how to make complaints about injustices or discrimination they have experienced.

Behaviour

The four schools involved in the project all found that a children's rights focus to teaching and learning had beneficial effects on the behaviour of children and their relationships with each other. This was as true in the playground as in the classroom.

At Torriano School, frictions that arose in the playground were discussed in the classroom. The children were encouraged to be assertive about what they wanted, working in groups and presenting their views to the class. These simple strategies helped children learn how to deal with difficult situations and showed the importance of dealing with the offence, rather than with the offender. Children learned to respect the rights of others, to take more responsibility for themselves and others and to express their needs and wants.

In research for the Commission for Racial Equality (1998) in which children's views were invited on how discipline could be improved, they suggested that teachers should:

- listen to pupils

- take trouble to sort out the underlying causes of disputes

- recognise bullying and racial and sexual name-calling as real problems among pupils

- care more about their pupils

- investigate allegations before they punish

- show respect for all pupils

Furthermore, the school should:

- find ways of canvassing pupils' views through suggestion boxes, questionnaires, assemblies and school newspapers

- invite parents to attend lessons

- train pupils in non-violent conflict resolution

- train pupils as counsellors

- discuss evaluations with pupils, allowing them to evaluate themselves and even their teacher

In the words of one pupil at Milverton County Primary School:

Since schools exist to educate children, shouldn't children be allowed to review their schools and teachers for Ofsted? Submission to the Children's Parliament

School Councils

Pupils need opportunities to take part in a range of decision-making activities and to be involved in the running of the school. For example, pupils can be representatives on school or class councils or on other school committees. (PSHE guidance, 2000)

Many schools now have a school council to give pupils a forum for their views. They demonstrate a great deal about how a representative democracy works, with children standing for election, campaigning through hustings, voting and, as council members, being accountable to their 'constituency' and standing up for the rights of their electorate. Questions about how younger children are represented on the council and how children with special needs are involved can provide profound lessons on the nature of citizenship and rights education for teachers and pupils alike.

Giving school councils teeth

Care has to be taken to ensure that school councils are more than decorative or tokenistic. In your school council:

- are the agenda and proceedings controlled by teachers?

- are councillors appointed by teachers?

- is its main function a talking shop, with no action taken on issues discussed?

In such circumstances, children could well learn that participation and democracy are a sham. Although it could be argued that a degree of cynicism in these matters is no bad thing, abuses of democratic systems deny children the right to make a positive contribution towards effective, democratic schools. Tokenistic practice led educationalist Rhys Griffith to observe:

WHY CHILDREN THINK IT IS IMPORTANT TO HAVE A SCHOOL COUNCIL

So the school improves and is much better organised.

Both girls and boys are involved.

Children know what is best for each other and it makes them happy.

If you didn't have one, you would have to do what the teachers say.

You get to have fun even though it is hard work.

To change the school in helpful ways.

The children get to decide what they want in the school.

If you didn't have one, then teachers wouldn't know what you want.

You set an example to younger children and some of the teachers, too.

You get to work with a team who is always thinking

From Sutton (1999)

I regard such practices [as pupil representation on committees and councils] as the doctrinaire inculcation of favoured pupils into the existing hierarchy of invested power. (Griffith, 1998)

Definition is the key to an effective school council. From the outset, clear lines should be drawn on the kind of issues it has jurisdiction over and what is beyond its remit.

One role for the school council might be as a consultative body for the head and staff, with the limits of its power and the reasons for them made known to the children. But while it's important to consider the boundaries of its scope carefully, teachers are often surprised at the maturity and good commonsense that children bring to their deliberations.

School Governors

The governing body has an important role to play in supporting a whole school approach to rights. It's within their remit to ensure adequate levels of funding to support this work, ensuring that staff have adequate and relevant training. Many governors will be well placed to help foster good relations between the school and local community. In addition, it gives staff a boost when governors take an active interest in teaching strategies, whether new or more traditional.

Links with parents and school communities

Save the Children's experience of working with school systems around the world has shown that schools can only be true communities when parents have strong participatory roles in relation to what is taught to their children and how it is done.

For parents to support the aims of the school, they need to be fully involved from the start. Teachers recognise the importance of affirming the home life of children even when they have to

challenge certain behaviours and attitudes. This is a sensitive area and confirms the need to have clear, easily understood policies in the relevant home languages that are fully communicated to parents. Home/school agreements, open evenings where parents experience 'taster' lessons and participate in cooperative problem-solving activities are all helpful. If parents understand what the school is trying to do, they are more likely to support it actively. At home children may be treated in ways that contradict what happens in school. Respecting parents doesn't mean that teachers have to acquiesce to all parents' views and opinions.

In their efforts to involve parents, some schools distribute questionnaires asking them for their views. When parents report that, for instance, it's difficult to find their way around the school or to talk to members of staff, responsive schools will put up signs and display photographs of all the adults who work in the school with captions saying what their role is.

Chapter Six

ASPECTS OF GLOBAL CITIZENSHIP

1. Children learning as world citizens

The model of education for citizenship which we brought to this research identifies four key elements for effective learning:

- *the acquisition of knowledge*

- *opportunities for reflecting on culture and identities*

- *the experience of living in a democratic community*

- *the development of skills for participation*

We see these four elements as the essential constituent parts of a wider programme of citizenship education and recognise that individual projects will not necessarily incorporate them all. (Osler and Starkey, 1999)

Children should learn their rights as an essential element of any course in citizenship. But as the quotation above notes, it may not be realistic for schools to expect to explore all the possibilities for young people learning to be citizens.

The Camden project:

provided knowledge about children's rights, particularly about the UN convention that upholds those rights

gave pupils opportunities to reflect on and share their own awareness of identities and the diversity of cultures within their classrooms and communities gave children the chance to gain experience in the nature of democratic communities through learning about or participating in school councils

gave scope for participation through, for instance, the 'Two Donkeys' problem-solving activity (page 38-39).

The Camden project also demonstrated ways in which learning for citizenship through rights could be further developed, notably by giving scope for reflection on a wider diversity of cultures. The Crick Commission Report on *Education for Citizenship and the Teaching of Democracy in Schools* maintained that primary schools are not centres of 'pre-citizenship learning' and neither should they be thought of as places for learning about only local and national aspects of citizenship. At key stages one and two, children can begin to understand their roles as global citizens. The Camden schools encouraged this understanding by choosing stories and traditions from many countries and cultures, from reading about Anancy the Caribbean spiderman to setting up mock Indian *panchayat* village councils. They explored the value of role-plays based on dilemmas in other cultures and created links with primary pupils in other parts of the world.

The good global citizen

When children are asked to draw their idea of a 'good citizen,' they are likely to depict aspects of social consciousness like picking up litter or helping old people across a road. In the classroom, pupils can be invited to take this further and more creatively by asking pupils to add visual aspects of good citizenship behaviour to a stick figure character by thinking how this ideal citizen uses his or her eyes, ears, hands, feet and so on.

If the word 'global' is then added to this activity, pupils generally find it harder to create a character because the range of experience now being asked about is so much wider. The usual res-

ponse to the initial task is to see the 'good citizen' as an active community member; in other words, at a local level. The idea of a good *global* citizen is likely to elicit responses which relate to conservation work or aspirations for world peace. They may possibly show some awareness of activities of the United Nations.

I think the greatest problem in the world today is war. Education can help to change that – improve people's attitudes towards each other. [translated from Spanish] William Mayta Quispe, age 13, Cusco, Peru – when asked about his hopes for the future. From *Class of 1999*, Save the Children, 1999.

Aspirations for future world peace and ecological protection may well be within teachers' classroom experience. However, official provisions for global citizenship learning in English schools are as yet scant and under-resourced. The Crick Report seems to make a distinction between learning about 'real' issues of democracy – participating at local and national levels – and an unspecified area of learning called 'awareness of world issues' beyond that. The report does, then, expect children to be aware and concerned about what is happening in the wider world beyond their classroom and their national borders. This is good. But it's not good enough.

The guidelines for PSHE at primary level scarcely advance on the Crick Report's position on global citizenship. Four learning objectives are recommended for 5 to 11 year olds:

– develop self-esteem, confidence, independence and responsibility and make the most of their abilities

– play an active role as future citizens and members of society

– develop a healthy lifestyle and keep safe

– develop effective and fulfiling relationships and learn to respect the differences between people

Children who are learning about their rights as citizens who participate in society and have their opinions valued should learn about more than their immediate world. Global citizenship education should mean that pupils are also learning to understand and use their roles for expression and change on a world scale.

The Crick Committee seems to see it as satisfactory for children merely to acquire knowledge of what is going on. But teachers and educators need to ask themselves 'whose knowledge?' and 'how do we learn about the world?' Without an approach centred on partnership and sharing on a larger scale, learning about the wider world will inevitably be restricted to a collection of facts identified and described by adults: teachers, writers of textbooks, news reporters, etc. The potential for learning from other children will be lost.

A view of citizenship education that allows far more scope to develop global citizenship awareness linked to local and national awareness comes from the QCA (1999) in guidance for secondary teachers:

> *Citizenship gives pupils the knowledge, skills and understanding to play an effective role in society at local, national and international levels. It helps them to become informed, thoughtful and responsible citizens who are aware of their duties and rights. It promotes their spiritual, moral, social and cultural development, making them more self-confident and responsible both in and beyond the classroom. It encourages pupils to play a helpful part in the life of their schools, neighbourhoods, communities and the wider world. It also... encourages respect for different national, regional and ethnic identities; and develops pupils' abilities to reflect on issues and take part in discussions.*

Three levels of 'society' are acknowledged in this statement and the world beyond the classroom is recognised. Although compulsory at secondary level alone, primary schools can build on this official guidance to construct courses that are global in scope.

The pedagogic problem appears to be more with learning what it means to be citizens of a nation. The two-ended model of local and global dimensions above needs to incorporate a 'middle' dimension of national citizenship to complete the picture. The Convention on the Rights of the Child advocates the 'development of respect for... the national values of the country in which the child is living' as part of the overall article on the democratic content of education (Article 29). Again, this is good but not good enough. The UK continues to be wary of educationally promoting national consciousness in contrast to countries that run civics courses concerned with national heroes, folklore, anthems, symbols of patriotism, etc.

The issue of national identity continues to be a vexed one, hijacked as it has been in this country by the extreme right. As well as history of 'non-European' civilisations being pared down in the history curriculum, the study of Britain since 1930 remains limited and open to criticism for its avoidance of matters around national sovereignty.

Recent moves towards decentralisation and the strengthening of separate identities with the new parliament in Scotland, the assembly in Wales and the restoration of the Stormont government in Northern Ireland should help clarify British nationhood on the one hand and confuse it on the other. Educators in England might find it easier to develop a sense of what it means to be English rather than British. Included in this debate is the contentious issue of minority cultural identity within a nation, be it English, Scottish, Welsh or Northern Irish. As Audrey Osler puts it:

Young citizens confident in their identities will be in a strong position to challenge the colonial and stereotypical images of minorities which currently help support discriminatory practices. Such a programme, based on human rights principles, has the potential to contribute to a new anti-racist project which will strengthen democratic institutions and practices and enable the full participation of all. (Osler, 2000)

Local and community level:

Citizenship involves learning about the four objectives for citizenship referred to above: confidence, active participation, health and effective relationships. Education for local citizenship can be pursued in school and out in the community. It can take the form of learning about caring for others through storytelling and it can be taught through geography or history-based local surveys for deeper understanding of how change works in communities.

National level:

Citizenship involves learning about national history from an inclusive perspective: the workers as well as the rulers, the minorities as well as the majority, women as well as men. National citizenship can include processes of voting and democracy as well as symbols of nationhood. It can and should extend to learning about the nature of nationalism itself and the dangers inherent in extreme forms of national self-expression.

Global level:

Citizenship involves learning about, with and from people in the wider contemporary world as well as in the past. World history can show children events from the perspectives of the vanquished and oppressed as well as of the victors and rulers. Books such as *The Vision of the Vanquished*, on South American historiography, aim to rebalance histories of the conquest from Spanish sources with what can be learnt from archaeology and extant sources of Aztec, Inca, Maya and other cultures.

World geography helps children analyse sources of information and evaluate places and environments from a variety of viewpoints. Through these different prisms they can see, for example, shanty town life through the eyes of the people who live there and contribute to township improvements as well as those who come from the outside to introduce their notions of 'quality of life.' They can gain insights into colonialism that fit so neatly into national curriculum studies on the Victorians. They can learn, too, how parallel civilisations, for instance in the Muslim world, were organised when western society was still relatively primitive.

Along with history and geography, learning as global citizens can include aspects of people's languages, literary heritage, art, music, dances, customs and traditions. The internet is an ideal vehicle for making contacts with pupils in other societies as well as learning about their countries.

Practical learning ideas for global citizenship

Learning from other cultures

Learning from other cultures means more than learning about the Kingdom of Benin or Indus Valley civilisations from secondary sources. An internationalist perspective on citizenship by definition demands:

> an interest in world cultures and a curiosity to find out more

> learning respect for cultures different from one's own

> regarding cultures as living and changing, affected by external circumstances such as invasion, colonisation, globalisation.

Learning through photography: an example

The Eye to Eye project is based in Palestinian refugee camps in Lebanon and the West Bank. Young people in the camps were given cameras and asked to record their perceptions of the com-

Asking questions about other cultures

Culture: What customs are celebrated in your community?

Community: What different groups of people are there?

Childhood: What is daily life like for the majority of young people?

Conflict: What makes people agree or disagree about change?

munities they live in. The result is a vivid resource showing authentic aspects of daily life in the camps and the young photographers' feelings and views about the present and the future.

Teachers can bring the experience of these young Palestinians into the classroom by using the Eye to Eye website. There is also a mobile exhibition of photographs available to schools. To complement Eye to Eye, pupils could participate in their own local photo-shoot to create a visual archive of daily life in their community.

International storytelling

Storytelling is an engaging, lively and pleasurable way of developing young people's sense of sharing and understanding of the lives of others.

We've already looked at different practical applications of classic stories like *Cinderella* and *The Little Red Hen* as a catalyst for discussion of shared values in the classroom. Such tales are part of children's universal inheritance.

Of course, children can create their own stories that serve to build up a group vision of values and experiences within the school. These in turn can be exchanged via email with children in other countries and cultures as a way of practising global citizenship.

One example of using storytelling to widen children's horizons is Save the Children's *Partners Project*, an education initiative in arts education linking the UK, Brazil, Cuba and Peru. In a back-street urban settlement in Recife, children at an Afro-Brazilian community centre told both traditional and modern stories as a group to an adult artist, who negotiated with them about which pictures and words would best suit the presentation of their stories and could be shared with other children beyond their own city and across the world, as a way of explaining culture and community.

In this example, the children's version of their cultural inheritance is vividly retold as the history of Capoeira (illustrated by Nara Menezes). (*Partners in Rights, creative activities exploring rights and citizenship for 7-11 year olds.* Save the Children, 2000).

Thinking globally, acting globally

Exploring rights documents with children, such as the Universal Declaration of Human Rights or the Convention on the Rights of the Child, can lead teachers to widen their remit onto an international level. Children may be interested to learn about the role of the United Nations or international welfare organisations concerned with peace-keeping or about refugee relief or the work of UNICEF. If pupils concentrate on a specific interest or join junior clubs or act as a class, they will move from factual knowledge towards citizenship in practice. Organisations like Friends of the Earth and GreenPeace, for example, provide a range of resources and activities, from information packs to practical action. Details of these and other organisations are given at the end of the book.

Direct exchanges

Setting up direct contact with young people outside the UK is supported by Article 13 of the Convention on the Rights of the Child, which recognises the right of every young person to...

seek, receive and impart information and ideas of all kinds, regardless of frontiers, either orally, in writing or in print, in the form of art, or through any other media of the child's choice.

Many schools have made successful links with schools on the Continent and beyond. Letters, worksheets, project folders and other documents, not to mention pupils and teachers themselves, have all travelled and been exchanged. In one link between primary schools in Scotland and Malawi, children chose and exchanged toys. The Malawian children learned to use Lego and the Scottish pupils learned to appreciate the skills required to make the spinning tops from wood and animal models from sun-dried clay that they had received in exchange.

The Global Footsteps project is another resource for teachers wanting to exchange learning about social and environmental issues with schools elsewhere in Europe, Africa, Asian and South America.

Even when direct links are not possible, it's important to nurture an understanding of the reality of the lives of others and avoid the kind of thinking behind the stereotypes of the developing and developed world. Discussions can be had on how young people can exercise their right to freedom of information exchanges regardless of frontiers – and what might be the obstacles for children to achieving this. Pupils will learn, in this way, to look beyond the clichés and stereotypes they find in the press, media and school textbooks and, hopefully, will be encouraged to ask questions about the reality behind the imagery.

The importance of language awareness

Evidence of other languages surrounds children in advertisements, on the television and in phrases coming into their own language. It's important for children to hear people speaking in their mother tongues and to recognise that the translation they are given may not be verbatim. Language awareness can be raised in class by role-play activities where different rules are created for different cultures and visitors have to work out how the community works. Learning to communicate in more than one language allows us to share information and experiences as world citizens. Children's home languages should be valued in the classroom, as much to uphold their cultural integrity as to make others aware that people express their ideas in a wide range of languages.

Conclusion

The teachers involved in this children's rights learning initiative grew into and with the project over the ten weeks during which it ran. As an experiment, it was a challenging process for teachers, pupils and the SC team. Taking on a rights agenda means, by definition, having to reassess your own attitudes and classroom management style and to confront your prejudices and insecurities. Some teachers found it harder than others to give children more of a voice than they usually had in what takes place in the classroom and how. For all of them, the experience of allowing pupils to take control initially meant taking a leap of faith. Some things worked and some didn't. Trying to disseminate their ideas and strategies to colleagues in the school was a major hurdle and all would admit that the project failed in that regard.

There was also an issue of time and curriculum constraints. As one teacher said, 'Even with getting cover for training and planning, I didn't have the time to map out things and then do them in a more considered way because there were just too many other things I had to do.'

But despite these difficulties, everyone involved in the project saw children's rights not only as an important component of citizenship but also as something that enhanced children's understanding of their entitlements as well as their self-esteem, communication skills and sense of their place in the world.

BIBLIOGRAPHY

ACE *Children's Voices in School Matters*. Report of an Advisory Centre for Education survey into school democracy. ACE Ltd., 1B Aberdeen Studios, 22 Highbury Grove, London N5 2DQ

Brown, Margot (ed) *Our World, Our Rights: Teaching about Rights and Responsibilities in the Primary School*. Amnesty International, 2000

Brownlie, Ali *Rights and Responsibilities*. Save the Children, 1998

Cattanach, Ann *Play Therapy: Where the Sky Meets the Underworld*. Jessica Kingsley, 1994.

Citizenship Foundation *You, Me, Us! Social and Moral Responsibility for Primary Schools*, edited by Don Rowe and Jan Newton. The Home Office, 1994

Colley, Linda *Britons: Forging the Nation 1707-1837*. Yale University Press, 1994

Commission for Racial Equality *Exclusion from School and Racial Equality*, CRE, 1998

Council of Europe *Teaching and Learning about Human Rights in Schools*. 1985

Crick, Bernard *Education for Citizenship and the Teaching of Democracy in Schools: Final Report of the Advisory Group for Citizenship Education (The Crick Report)*. QCA, 1998

Cuninghame, Christopher (ed) *Realising Children's Rights: Policy, Practice and Save the Children's Work in England*. Save the Children, 1999

Derman-Sparkes, Louise and the ABC Task Force *The Anti-Bias Curriculum: Tools for Empowering Young Children*. NAEYC, 1989

Development Education Association (1) Citizenship Education in a Global Context. *The Development Education Journal* Vol. 6, October 1999

Development Education Association (2) Global Perspectives in the National Curriculum, Human Rights, Guidance for Key Stages 2 and 3. *The Development Education Journal* Vol. 6, October 1999

Development Education Association (3) Citizenship Education in a Global Context. *The Development Education Journal* Vol. 6, October 1999

Development Education Centre, Birmingham *Start with a Story*. DEC Birmingham, 1991

Dixon, Annabelle, Citizenship in the Early Years? *Co-ordinate*, 1998

Farrington, Lorna *Changing Our School, Promoting Positive Behaviour*. London Institute of Education, 1997

Fountain, Susan *Learning Together, Global Education 4-7*. Stanley Thornes, 1990

Fountain, Susan *Only Right*. UNICEF, 1993

Griffin, Helen and Ballin, Ben, Building Blocks for Global Learning. *Global Education*, 1999

Griffith, Rhys *Educational Citizenship and Independent Learning*. Jessica Kingsley, 1998

Harding, Sheila and Unwin, Rob *Developing Rights: Teaching about rights and responsibilities for ages 11-14*. Oxfam, 1999

Hart, R. *Children's Participation*. Earthscan, 1999

Holden, Cathie and Clough, Nick (eds) *Children as Citizens: Education for Participation*. Jessica Kingsley, 1998

Institute of Education London *Involving Pupils*. Research Matters, 1997

Kennedy, K.J. *Citizenship Education and the Modern State*. Falmer Press, 1997

Kenner, Charmian *Learning Together: Experiences of Family Learning in Hackney Schools*. Hackney Learning Partnerships, 2000

Lansdown, Gerison, Progress in Implementing the Rights in the UN Convention on the Rights of the Child. Paper delivered at the International Conference on Children's Rights and Education, 1998

Mackenzie, J.M. *Propaganda and Empire: the manipulation of British public opinion 1880-1960*. Manchester University Press, 1984

Miller, Judy *Never Too Young*. National Early Years Network and Save the Children, 1997

Osler, A and Starkey H, Rights, Identities and Inclusion: European action programmes as political education. *Oxford Review of Education*, Vol. 25, Nos. 1 and 2, 1999

Osler, A, The Crick Report: difference, equality and racial justice. *Curriculum Journal* Vol. 11 No. 1, Spring 2000

Pandrich, Christine (ed) *We Have Rights Okay, Children's Views of the United Nations Convention on the Rights of the Child*. SC England Programme Office, 1999

Pickering, J *Involving Pupils in Research Matters*. London Institute of Education, 1997

QCA (1) *Framework for personal, social and health education and citizenship at key stages 1 and 2 in the National Curriculum Handbook for primary teachers in England*. DfEE and QCA, 1999

QCA (2) *Citizenship at key stages 3 and 4 in The National Curriculum Handbook for secondary teachers in England*. DfEE and QCA, 1999

QCA (3) *Personal, social and health education and citizenship at key stages 1 and 2, Initial guidance for schools, consultation draft*. January 2000

Richardson, Robin and Wood, Angela *Inclusive Schools, Inclusive Society: Race and Identity on the Agenda*. ROTA, Save the Children and Trentham Books 1999

Rowe, Don, *Introducing Citizenship: a handbook for primary schools*. A&C Black, 2001

Save the Children/UNICEF *Rights of the Child topic books: The Whole Child; It's Our Right; Keep Us Safe* with teachers' handbook. SC/UNICEF 1990

Save the Children *Changing Childhoods: Britain since 1930: a sourcebook for learning about children and social change with 8 to 12 year olds*. SC 1996

Save the Children *We Have Rights Okay: a report on the UN Convention on the Rights of the Child*. SC 1999

Save the Children *Class of 1999 World's Children*. SC 1999

Save the Children *Partners in Rights, creative activities exploring rights and citizenship for 7-11 year olds*. Based on children's experiences in the UK, Latin America and the Caribbean, SC 2000

Save the Children with Leeds Development Education Centre Families Pack: *Activities and photographs to raise moral, social, cultural and spiritual issues in PSHE and citizenship for key stages 1 and 2*. SC 1999

School Councils Charitable Trust School *Councils Councils Starter Pack* 2000

Steiner, Miriam *Learning from Experience: World Studies in the Primary Curriculum*. Trentham Books, 1993

Sutton, Faye *The School Council: a Children's Guide*. Save the Children, 1999

UNICEF *UN Convention on the Rights of the Child*. Set of posters.

United Nations *The Convention on the Rights of the Child*. UN 1989

Walkington, Helen *Global Citizenship Education*. The Geographical Association 1999

Warren, David and Christie, Donald *Teaching Social Behaviour: classroom activities to foster children's interpersonal awareness*. David Fulton

Wilkes, S *One Day We Had to Run*. Evans Bros. in association with UNHCR and Save the Children 1997

Advisory Centre for Education (ACE)
1B Aberdeen Studios
22 Highbury Grove
London N5 2DQ
0207 354 8321
Supports and gives advice on children's rights in and out of school.

Amnesty International
99-119 Rosebery Avenue
London EC1R 4RE
Tel: 0207 814 6200
www.amnesty.org
Has schools pages on website featuring information and activities reflecting its international human rights work.

Article 12
8 Wakley Street
London EC1V 7QE
An organisation run by and for children and young people under the age of 18 which aims to ensure that children have a right to express their views and have them taken seriously.

Children's Legal Centre
University of Essex
Wivenhoe Park
Colchester, Essex CO4 3SQ
Offers free legal advice and information to children and young people.

Children's Play Council
cpc@ncb.org.uk
Promotes the importance of consultation with children and young people and stimulates partnerships between play and other children's services.

Children's Rights Information Network
www.crin.org
Global network of children's rights organisations, set up for the purpose of exchanging information and promoting implementation of the UN Convention on the Rights of the Child.

UNIVERSITY OF HERTFORDSHIRE LRC

Children's Rights Office
319 City Road
London ECV 1LJ
0207 278 8222

Citizenship Foundation
15 St Swithins Lane
London EC4
Tel: 0207 929 3344
A leading pioneer in citizenship education, producing excellent classroom and teachers' materials.

Eye to Eye website
savethechildren.org.uk/eyetoeye/main.html

Friends of the Earth
26-28 Underwood Street
London N1 7JQ
Tel: 0207 490 0881
Working for solutions to environmental problems.

Greenpeace
Canonbury Villas
London N1 2PN
Tel: 0207 865 8100
International environmental activist organisation.

Human Rights International Alliance
30a Chertsey Road
Woking, Surrey GU21 5AJ
www.hria.net
Works for and produces information on children's rights.

Human Rights Internet
www.hri.ca
Large website with links to worldwide human rights organisations and projects including children's rights.

Institute for Citizenship
62 Marylebone High St.
London W1
Tel: 0207 935 4777

London Children's Rights Commissioner
94 White Lion Street,
London N1
infoteam@londonchildrenscommissioner.org.uk
Runs a number of projects including Sort it Out, children's ideas for building a better London and a report on the State of London's Children, research an statistics showing a picture of childhood in London today. The Commissioner is working with the Greater London Assembly to develop London's first children's strategy.

National Early Years Network
77 Holloway Road
London N7 8JZ

Refugee Council
Head Office: Bondway
London SW8 1SJ
The largest organisation in the UK working with asylum seekers and refugees.

Save the Children Centre for Young Children's Rights
356 Holloway Road
London N7
Tel: 0207 700 8127
www.scuk.org.uk
Contains a resource centre with classroom materials to support children's rights education.

School Councils UK Charitable Trust
57 Etchingham Park Road
London N3 2EB
Tel: 0208 349 2459
www.SchoolCouncils.org

UNICEF
55 Lincoln's Inn Fields
London WC2A 3NB
Tel: 0207 405 5592
www.unicef.org
Works for the protection of children's rights. Has web pages on the UN Convention aimed at schools.

362913

DH

372.
832
044
094
1
KLE

6000486966